PUFFIN BOOKS

THE PUFFIN TRIVIA QUIZ GAME BOOK

Whether you're bright and brainy or a real dumbo, you've got what it takes to play a Trivia game! Your head is stuffed full of trivial bits of knowledge, which you have acquired over the years, and they're just waiting to be let out. Here's your chance to be a mastermind.

The Puffin Trivia Quiz Game Book has been created especially for children. Complete with the games from *The Ultimate Trivia Quiz Game Book* (Penguin), it can be used on car journeys or in other idle moments with family and friends – or just simply for driving adults wild! There are pop questions, book questions, film questions, science questions – every kind of question you can imagine (with a liberal helping of trick questions), which will leave you either triumphant or weeping with frustration as an answer hovers on the tip of your tongue!

Maureen Hiron is perhaps best known as a games inventor. Creator of the best-selling Continuo and Quizwrangle games, she teamed up with her husband, Alan, to write the best-selling *Ultimate Trivia Quiz Game Book*. David Elias began his career in quizzes as a competitor in several TV and radio quiz shows, including *The Krypton Factor*.

The Puffin Trivia Quiz Game Book

Maureen and Alan Hiron and David Elias

Illustrated by Tony Blundell

PUFFIN BOOKS

PUFFIN BOOKS

Published by the Penguin Group
27 Wrights Lane, London w8 5TZ, England
Viking Penguin Inc., 40 West 23rd Street, New York, New York 10010, USA
Penguin Books Australia Ltd, Ringwood, Victoria, Australia
Penguin Books Canada Ltd, 2801 John Street, Markham, Ontario, Canada L3R 1B4
Penguin Books (NZ) Ltd, 182–190 Wairau Road, Auckland 10, New Zealand

Penguin Books Ltd. Registered Offices: Harmondsworth, Middlesex, England

First published 1985
Reprinted 1986 (three times), 1988

Printed in Great Britain by
Richard Clay Ltd, Bungay, Suffolk
Typeset in Linotron Aldus by
Rowland Phototypesetting Ltd, Bury St Edmunds, Suffolk

Introduction

by Alan Hiron

Learning can be as dull as ditchwater – do you really remember (or care) which king succeeded Henry V and in which year? Or what is the main export of Zambia?

These are not facts that stick easily in your mind. But if asked, 'From which country did the pop-group ABBA come?' (Sweden) most of you would get it right. Can you see what I mean? Even while writing this I have forgotten who succeeded Henry V. (Was it Henry VI – or did one of the Richards come next?) Is copper the main Zambian export? I'm not sure without looking it up.

One of the fun things about this book is that you can argue about the answers while you are playing the games. For example, 'In the story of *Peter Pan*, how many fingers did Captain Hook have?' you could reason that he must have had the full ration to start with, but at the time of the story he only had one arm, therefore, five fingers, or four fingers and one thumb. In a curious way, any arguments you have about the answers help you remember the facts.

There is another oddity. Don't feel that collecting all sorts of strange (and often useless) knowledge will mean that you won't remember the more important things in life – from the textbooks that you need for examinations and so on which are much less fun. It works in quite the other way – the more used your brain is to collecting and storing information, the easier it finds it!

As far as playing the book is concerned, you can either play any of the suggested games with your friends or play on equal terms with your parents. You sound surprised? No, you ask them questions from Penguin's *The Ultimate Trivia Quiz Game Book* or from *Beyond The Ultimate Trivia Quiz Game Book* and they ask you questions from this one.

How to Play the Book

All answers are on the following left-hand page, overleaf, so that there is no need to grub around the back of the book. Nor is there any need to turn back, unless your questionee has forgotten the question. Keep going through the book in numerical order. Even if only one question is answered from each quiz, ask the next contestant a question from the following quiz. This eliminates cheating. Only when you have reached Quiz 88 do you return to the beginning of the book, to start again with Quiz 89. In the fullness of time, you may be lucky enough to be asked a question that you or someone else has had before – and you might even remember the answer!

All the Trivia Quizzes contain nine questions. They are roughly grouped into the following categories, which remain the same throughout the book:

1. Ragbag
2. Mainly historical
3. Mainly geographical
4. Literature, mythology and the Bible
5. Sport
6. Entertainment
7. Leisure, people and art
8. Music, in all its manifestations
9. Loosely, science and natural history

So, if you choose or are given question 5, be prepared for sport.

Following are some of the games that you can play competitively, between individuals or teams. Game charts are provided.

Some hints on equipment

If you haven't got any dice or, for Quizwrangle, the rather special ten-sided dice which are not readily available in the shops, then you can easily find an alternative way of selecting question numbers. For Quizwrangle, take a pack of cards and remove the kings, queens and jacks. Shuffle the remaining forty cards and simply turn up the top three for the first player (10 counts as zero in Quizwrangle). Any rejects are put in a discard pile and new cards taken from the top of the pack (this is the equivalent of rerolling dice). Only when the stockpile is finished are the cards reshuffled and used again.

Similarly, if you are playing a game such as 'Onwards, Ever Onwards' that needs only six categories, you can sort out the appropriate twenty-four cards and use them in the same way. Use two packs if you like; not everyone has dice in the house, but a pack of cards is usually within range.

Onwards, Ever Onwards

Equipment needed   This book; 1 standard six-sided die; a distinguishing marker for each player.

All players place their marker on the *Start* square. Decide the order of play. Then each player throws the die and moves his or her marker the number of squares shown on the die, following the direction of the arrows. If you land on a zero your turn is over, and the die passes to the next contestant. Land on any other number, and an opponent asks you the question appropriate to that number from the next quiz. If you answer correctly you retain the die and throw again, and continue to do so until you answer incorrectly or land on a zero, when your turn ends.

To win   You *must* answer a question that takes you on to or past the *Finish* square. You *cannot* win just by throwing the die and galloping past the post.

Note   In theory, you could win without your opponents ever getting their paws on the die; but it won't happen – well, it hasn't yet.

	7 → 8		0 → 6		4 → 5		2 → 3		0
1	6	9	5	7	3	0	1	4	9
2	0	0	4	8	2	6	0	5	8
3	5	1	3	9	1	7	9	0	7
4	4	2	2	0	0	8	8	6	6
5	3	3	1	1	9	9	7	7	0
0	2	4	0	2	8	0	6	8	5
6	1	5	9	3	7	1	0	9	4
7	0	0	8	4	6	2	5	0	3
8 → 9		6 → 7		5 → 0		3 → 4		1 → 2

ONWARDS, EVER ONWARDS

9

Quizwrangle

Quizwrangle was Britain's first Trivia game, devised by the authors of this tome. It has become quite a cult, and the constant requests for even more questions from Quizwrangle *aficionados* provided the inspiration for this book, which can also be used in conjunction with Quizwrangle.

Equipment needed　This book; 3 decahedral (ten-sided) dice; 9 counters.

Quizwrangle is played between two individuals or two teams of players. Place the board so that the dark squares at each end face the players. Place one counter on each of the central numbered spaces. Teams take turns to roll the three dice: either the original numbers may be accepted, or the player can reroll one, two or all three dice – but only one reroll is allowed. (Have you ever played poker dice? It's the same idea.)

You automatically move your counter one square towards you in the lanes indicated by the numbers on the dice. If you throw a zero, tough – you miss a question!

Now your opponents will ask you questions from the appropriate numbers. If you answer correctly, move an extra square towards you in that lane; if you answer incorrectly, stay where you are.

If your dice include the same number two or three times, you only get to answer the question once – but if you answer correctly, you move *two* extra squares in the appropriate lane, rather than the usual one, if *two* dice show the same number, and *three* extra squares if all *three* dice show the same number.

Continue on to the next quiz after each player or team has had a turn.

In order to nullify the advantage of having the first roll, the team or player which starts rolls only two dice and is not permitted a reroll. After this, all three dice are used throughout by both sides.

To win The game is won by the first player or team to get three (or four – decide *before* play begins) counters into the dark squares nearest to them. It's rather like nine simultaneous tugs-of-war.

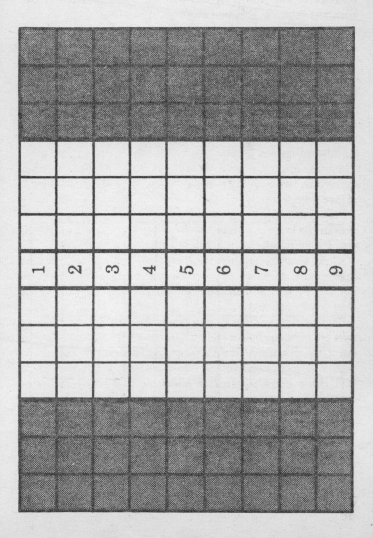

Tic Tac Trivia

For two or more players or teams.

How to win   Get your initials, or other distinguishing feature, in a consecutive row of three, horizontally, vertically or diagonally.

How to play   Choose any section. Another player asks the question, and if you answer correctly, place your mark in any space along the line of that section only. One question per turn, and play passes in rotation. There is no penalty for a wrong answer.

Note   It can pay to defend as well as attack!

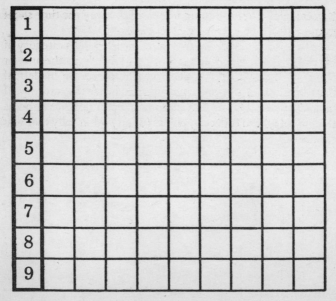

Count-up

For any number of players.

Equipment needed   A pack of cards with kings, queens, jacks and 10s removed; scorepad.

First decide the order of play. Then shuffle the cards and place them face down. Each player turns up the top card and is asked the question relating to the number on that card from the next quiz. Score 1 point for each correct answer. The first player to reach 10 points wins (or any other number of points that you agree upon *before* play starts).

Trivel Travia

You can play a very simple game to while away the time spent in travelling by car, train, coach or plane.

In turn, each player has the option of selecting a category of his choice – for which he scores 1 point if he gets the answer right – or allowing the opposition (the player on his left, if there are more than two contestants) to choose the category. If the player gets this one right, he scores 2 points. The winner is the first player to collect 15 points (or any other tally that you choose).

Get Out of That

Equipment needed This book; a small distinguishing marker for each player.

For any number of players.

All players place their markers in the centre circle. Each player is asked question 1 in turn – not question 1 from the same quiz: plough on through the book. (There is an advantage to being quizzed early, so we suggest that you cut a pack of cards to determine the order of play.)

If you answer correctly, move your marker one space outwards on the circle to any number, even if there is already someone else's marker on it. If you answer incorrectly, stay put, and have another go at category 1 when it is your turn again.

The procedure for the next round is as follows. If you have moved, you must now correctly answer a question from the category whose number you are occupying, so that you can continue your journey outwards. You may choose which of the two adjoining numbers to move on to, but once you've moved, you cannot change your mind. That is the category on which you will next be quizzed in the next round. If you answer incorrectly, you remain where you are until your next turn, when you will be asked another question from the same category.

The first player to reach the *Winner's Enclosure* is the winner.

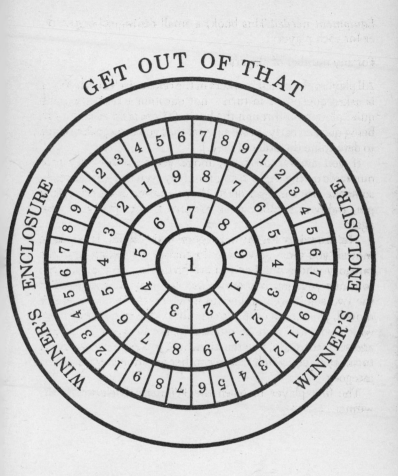

1. What would you see exhibited at Cruft's?
2. Who was the famous queen of the Iceni who led her tribe in battles against the Romans?
3. If you sailed on a boat through Cairo, on which river would you be?
4. In the story of *Peter Pan*, how many fingers did Captain Hook have?
5. Who is Nicky Slater's ice-dancing partner?
6. Who asks the questions on television's daily quiz for teenagers, *Blockbusters*?
7. For what did Cole Porter, George Gershwin and Jerome Kern become famous?
8. From which country did the pop group ABBA come?
9. Two otters, two peewits and a spider – how many legs altogether?

1. Tap, break and Latin-American are all styles of what?
2. How many wives did King Henry VIII have?
3. On which island are the towns of Douglas, Peel and Ramsey?
4. What's the name of Sherlock Holmes's faithful friend?
5. With which sport do you connect Jocky Wilson and Eric Bristow?
6. What's the name of the character played by George Peppard who's the leader of the 'A-Team'?
7. With what sort of transport do you associate Evel Knievel, Barry Sheen and Ron Haslam?
8. Who used to be the partner of singer Art Garfunkel until they began separate careers?
9. Which teacher of deaf people invented the telephone?

1

1. Pedigree dogs.
2. Boudicca, or Boadicea.
3. The Nile.
4. Five, or four and a thumb.
5. Karen Barber.
6. Bob Holness.
7. Composing songs.
8. Sweden.
9. Twenty.

89

1. Dancing.
2. Six.
3. The Isle of Man.
4. Doctor Watson.
5. Darts.
6. Colonel Hannibal Smith.
7. The motorcycle.
8. Paul Simon.
9. Alexander Graham Bell.

1. There are two archbishops in the Church of England. One is Canterbury – who is the other?
2. Which American president was shot dead in a theatre in 1865?
3. Which country is called Nippon, or the Land of the Rising Sun?
4. Who wrote the stories *Carrie's War* and *The Peppermint Pig*?
5. Berm, table-top and bunny-hop are terms used in which sport?
6. Who asks the questions on the celebrity game show *Punchlines*?
7. In which pantomime story would you expect to see Buttons and the Ugly Sisters?
8. Which group had a number one pop hit in 1985 with 'You Spin Me Round'?
9. Which name meaning 'terrible lizard' is used to describe some prehistoric creatures?

1. Lymeswold and Stilton are kinds of what?
2. Which king of England was the grandfather of Queen Elizabeth II?
3. Which large lake in Scotland is believed by some people to contain a huge monster?
4. A centaur in mythology was half man and half what?
5. In the Oxford and Cambridge boat race, how many people are in each boat?
6. Which ex-teacher asks the questions on the TV quiz based on darts, *Bullseye*?
7. Which famous politician has twin children called Carol and Mark?
8. Which pedal on a piano should you press to help you play more quietly?
9. Which science may be organic or inorganic?

2

1. York.
2. Abraham Lincoln.
3. Japan.
4. Nina Bawden.
5. BMX bike-riding.
6. Lenny Bennett.
7. Cinderella.
8. Dead or Alive.
9. Dinosaur.

90

1. Cheese.
2. George V.
3. Loch Ness.
4. Horse.
5. Nine – eight rowers and the cox.
6. Jim Bowen.
7. Mrs Margaret Thatcher.
8. The left one.
9. Chemistry.

1. What sort of job does a QC usually do?
2. In which year did the First World War begin?
3. How many states are there in the USA?
4. Who wrote *The Secret Diary of Adrian Mole, Aged 13¾*?
5. Which sport begins with a 'bully' and uses a hard white ball?
6. Which ex-teacher asks the questions on the TV quiz show based on playing cards, *Gambit*?
7. Of which country was Mrs Indira Gandhi the prime minister until she was assassinated in 1984?
8. Which group made the successful LP 'Welcome to the Pleasure Dome'?
9. Which American firm manufactures the 747 jumbo jet?

1. Of which tree does a koala bear eat the leaves?
2. Which nation attacked Pearl Harbor without warning in 1941?
3. In which country is the state of New South Wales?
4. What did the gorgon, Medusa, wear on her head instead of hair?
5. In which game do players aim woods at a jack?
6. Who is the presenter of the TV game show *Child's Play*, and used to present *Give Us A Clue*?
7. What was the first name of the famous Spanish painter Picasso, who died in 1973?
8. Which instrument – in this case made of gold – does James Galway play?
9. Which animals were the dogs called dachshunds bred to hunt?

3

1. He or she is a lawyer – either a barrister or a judge.
2. 1914.
3. Fifty.
4. Sue Townsend.
5. Field hockey.
6. Tom O'Connor.
7. India.
8. Frankie Goes to Hollywood.
9. Boeing.

A jumbo jet?

91

1. The eucalyptus.
2. Japan.
3. Australia.
4. Snakes.
5. Bowls.
6. Michael Aspel.
7. Pablo.
8. The flute.
9. Badgers. Dachshund means 'badger hound' in German.

Which animals were dachshunds bred to hunt?

1. Which small yellow bird is Snoopy's friend in the cartoon strip?
2. How many of Henry VIII's wives were beheaded?
3. Which country was once ruled by kaisers?
4. Who wrote the children's books *Grinny*, *Monster Maker* and *Space Hostages*?
5. Which American player has won a record twenty Wimbledon titles?
6. What's the name of the popular television series about highway patrol motorcyclists from California?
7. Who was the painter of the famous smiling portrait, the 'Mona Lisa'?
8. Who wrote the music for *Evita* and *Cats*?
9. Where in the human body would you find molars and bicuspids?

1. What do the letters UFO mean when used to describe a strange thing in the sky?
2. Which explorer sailed in a ship called the *Pelican* in 1577?
3. Which two countries are separated by the River Niagara and the Niagara Falls?
4. Which artist and author's books include *Fungus the Bogeyman*, *The Snowman* and *Father Christmas*?
5. For which country did the footballer George Best win thirty-seven international caps?
6. Who reads the stories about *Thomas the Tank Engine and Friends* on television?
7. Which toys that you can't buy, only adopt, were invented by Xavier Roberts?
8. Which great composer's middle name was Amadeus?
9. What do you call a three-dimensional picture produced by laser light?

4

1. Woodstock.
2. Two: Anne Boleyn and Catherine Howard.
3. Germany.
4. Nicholas Fisk.
5. Billie-Jean King.
6. *CHIPS*.
7. Leonardo da Vinci.
8. Andrew Lloyd Webber.
9. In your mouth – they're teeth.

92

1. Unidentified Flying Object.
2. Sir Francis Drake.
3. Canada and the USA.
4. Raymond Briggs.
5. Northern Ireland.
6. Ringo Starr.
7. The Cabbage Patch Kids.
8. Wolfgang Amadeus Mozart.
9. A hologram.

1. Before British money was decimalized in 1971, how many pennies were there in a shilling?
2. Which king of England was nicknamed 'the Confessor'?
3. If Bonn is the capital of West Germany, what's the capital of East Germany?
4. Who wrote the children's books about the Bagthorpe family, Lizzie Dripping and Jumbo Spencer?
5. Which ball game is played with a stick that has a triangular net at one end?
6. Who is the large-size host of *On Safari* who also appears on *Surprise, Surprise!*?
7. What's the name of the daughter of actors Debbie Reynolds and Eddie Fisher who played Princess Leia in *Star Wars*?
8. To which group do Mikey Craig and drummer Jon Moss belong?
9. With which instrument does a doctor listen to your chest?

1. Which street in London is famous as the home of many daily newspapers?
2. Who was Queen Victoria's husband?
3. Through which capital city does the River Seine flow?
4. What sort of animal is Babar in Jean de Brunhoff's books?
5. What do you call the rubber disc used in ice hockey instead of a ball?
6. What's the name of the TV show, made up of four initial letters, that stars Paul Henley, Anneka Rice and Paul Shearer?
7. How many children has Queen Elizabeth II?
8. In which group does Stewart Copeland play drums and Andy Summers guitar?
9. Which famous scientist's picture appeared on a British £1 note?

5

1. Twelve.
2. Edward.
3. Berlin.
4. Helen Cresswell.
5. Lacrosse.
6. Christopher Biggins.
7. Carrie Fisher.
8. Culture Club.
9. A stethoscope.

93

1. Fleet Street.
2. Prince Albert.
3. Paris.
4. An elephant.
5. A puck.
6. CBTV.
7. Four.
8. Police.
9. Sir Isaac Newton.

1. What would a cockney mean if he referred to a whistle in rhyming slang?
2. Which British prime minister had the first names William Ewart?
3. Which country's red and white flag carries a maple leaf?
4. Who wrote the children's books *Smith*, *Black Jack* and *Devil-in-the-Fog*?
5. How many more players are on the field in a rugby union game than in rugby league?
6. Which television quiz is based on the game Battleships, with Richard Stilgoe asking the questions?
7. What's the title of the popular ITV programme about people's holidays, introduced by Chris Kelly and Judith Chalmers?
8. Which dancer asks the questions on 'Name That Tune'?
9. Which bird that can fly has the largest wing span?

1. What's the name of the memory game involving looking at a large number of objects for a short time, then trying to list them?
2. Who built the 'Rocket', a steam locomotive, in 1829?
3. To which country do the Balearic islands (including Ibiza) belong?
4. In Barbara Euphan Todd's books, who was 'The Scarecrow of Scatterbrook Farm'?
5. The Irish game of hurling is very like which British team game?
6. On which programme does Eamonn Andrews surprise people with his 'big red book'?
7. Which famous soldier was nicknamed 'the Iron Duke'?
8. What's the surname of the singer Toyah?
9. What could be called cirrostratus or altocumulus?

6

1. Suit – it rhymes with 'whistle and flute'.
2. Gladstone.
3. Canada.
4. Leon Garfield.
5. Four – two more on each side.
6. *Finders Keepers*.
7. *Wish You Were Here* . . .
8. Lionel Blair.
9. The wandering albatross.

94

1. Kim's Game.
2. George Stephenson.
3. Spain.
4. Worzel Gummidge.
5. Hockey.
6. *This Is Your Life*.
7. The Duke of Wellington.
8. Wilcox.
9. They are kinds of clouds.

1. What's the exact date of St Valentine's Day?
2. Which city is said to have been founded by Romulus and Remus?
3. What's the largest island belonging to Greece?
4. Which hero of mythology rescued Andromeda from a sea serpent?
5. In a three-day event, what name is given to the complicated exercises done by horse and rider on the first day?
6. In which programme does actor David Hasselhoff drive a car called KITT?
7. Which Italian inventor was the first man to send a message across the Atlantic by radio?
8. Which great composer's middle name was Sebastian?
9. Where in your body is a bone called a patella?

1. Where would you see a Plimsoll line painted?
2. Which famous tapestry tells the story of how the Normans invaded Britain in 1066?
3. In which country is the famous tomb called the Taj Mahal?
4. In Clive King's book, which Stone Age friend of Barney lives in a chalk pit in Kent?
5. What sort of sport has varieties called skeet, Olympic trench and down-the-line?
6. Where do Bungle, Zippy, George and Thumbelina appear together?
7. Why might a speleologist enjoy visiting the Cheddar Gorge?
8. Cheryl Baker, Jay Aston, Mike Noland and Bobby Gee formed which group of singers?
9. Black widow, trapdoor and wolf are kinds of what?

7

1. The fourteenth of February.
2. Rome.
3. Crete.
4. Perseus.
5. Dressage.
6. *Knight Rider*.
7. Guglielmo Marconi.
8. Johann Sebastian Bach.
9. Patella is the Latin word for knee-cap.

Complicated exercises by horse and rider

95

1. On the side of a ship.
2. The Bayeux Tapestry.
3. India.
4. Stig, in *Stig of the Dump*.
5. Shooting at clay pigeons.
6. In *Rainbow*, on television.
7. He's interested in caves.
8. Buck's Fizz.
9. Spider.

1. What's the name of the official residence of the president of the USA?
2. On which ship did the Pilgrim Fathers sail to America in 1620?
3. What's the present-day name of the ancient city of Constantinople?
4. Who are Dick, Julian, Anne, George and Timmy the dog?
5. Which sport would you expect to see the Harlem Globetrotters play?
6. At which number do Ethel, Dawn, Neil and Harry welcome TV viewers on Saturday mornings?
7. What were Virgil and Dante famous for doing?
8. What's the rest of the name of the Liverpool pop group, Echo and . . . ?
9. Fish don't have lungs, so how do they breathe?

1. At which meal would a Frenchman be most likely to eat croissants?
2. What was the name of the English king nicknamed Rufus?
3. Which country's flag is green and white, with a red dragon?
4. In the Bible, who is the father of Cain and Abel?
5. Old Trafford is the home ground of which football team?
6. Which live TV talent show has Tim Brooke-Taylor and Stan Boardman as hosts, and an 'electronic hook'?
7. Who is the famous sister of Viscount Althorp?
8. Which letter on a piece of music tells a performer to play loudly?
9. What do the letters VHF stand for in broadcasting?

8

1. The White House.
2. The *Mayflower*.
3. Istanbul.
4. The Famous Five in the stories by Enid Blyton.
5. Basketball.
6. Number 73.
7. Writing poetry.
8. Echo and the Bunnymen.
9. Through their gills.

Fish don't have lungs . . .

96

1. Breakfast.
2. William II.
3. Wales.
4. Adam.
5. Manchester United.
6. *The Fame Game*.
7. Diana, Princess of Wales.
8. It is *f*, standing for *forte*.
9. Very High Frequency.

1. In American money, how many nickels make one dime?
2. What name was given to the campaigners for votes for women who sometimes chained themselves to railings in protest?
3. What's the largest island that belongs to Italy?
4. What sort of creatures are General Woundwort, Hazel, Fiver and Blackberry?
5. In show jumping, how many penalty points, or faults, does a horse score if it knocks down both parts of a double fence?
6. What does Leslie Crowther say first to contestants on *The Price is Right*?
7. In the number one hit, Nena sang about ninety-nine what?
8. Ringo, Frog, JT, Charley and Sniffer are the nicknames of which pop group?
9. If veins take blood to your heart, which blood vessels take it away again?

1. What is a klaxon?
2. How much was a guinea worth in today's money?
3. The Argentines call them Malvinas. What do we call them?
4. In mythology, if you look at a gorgon, what happens to you?
5. Over what distance did Mike McLeod of Britain take 28 minutes and 6.22 seconds to win an Olympic silver medal in 1984?
6. Which policeman, who trains other policemen, is played on TV by William Shatner?
7. What was the surname of the hero of the American west, Buffalo Bill?
8. In the song about the twelve days of Christmas, how many gold rings are given?
9. What's the name of the piece of wire inside an electric light bulb that glows to give out light?

9

1. Two.
2. They were called suffragettes.
3. Sicily.
4. Rabbits, in *Watership Down*.
5. Eight.
6. Come on down!
7. Red balloons.
8. Duran Duran.
9. The arteries.

97

1. A loud horn or hooter.
2. £1.05, previously 21 shillings.
3. The Falkland Islands.
4. You turn to stone.
5. 10,000 metres.
6. T. J. Hooker.
7. Cody.
8. Five.
9. The filament.

1. Who has a weekend home called Chequers?
2. What was the surname of the Scottish outlaw Rob Roy?
3. Which country used to be called Abyssinia?
4. Who travels to Brobdingnag on his second voyage?
5. To break the world pole-vault record, how high (to the nearest metre) would you have to vault?
6. Which serial is set in Fulley comprehensive school with characters called Megapig and Trolley Molly?
7. For which of the arts are Barbara Hepworth and Henry Moore famous?
8. Which singer with the Boomtown Rats organized the Ethiopian famine appeal through Band Aid?
9. What does a tiny young animal called a joey grow up to be?

1. Which word can mean both a noisy row and an object used for hitting a ball?
2. In which war did Prince Rupert fight the Ironsides?
3. In which country is Sarajevo, where the 1984 Winter Olympics were held?
4. For what achievement is the Bible character Methuselah particularly famous?
5. In which sport might a player call out 'Fore!' to warn spectators?
6. Which series about children's reading has been introduced by Tom Baker and by Neil Innes?
7. Who is now the operator of Sooty and Sweep, the puppets invented by his father?
8. Which musical instrument do you associate with Richard Clayderman?
9. Which breed of dog is the heaviest?

10

1. The prime minister of Great Britain.
2. Macgregor.
3. Ethiopia.
4. Lemuel Gulliver.
5. 6 metres. The 1984 record was 5.90 metres.
6. *Behind the Bike Sheds*.
7. Sculpture.
8. Bob Geldof.
9. Kangaroo.

98

1. Racket.
2. The English Civil War.
3. Yugoslavia.
4. Living to the great age of 969, although it was probably 969 months!
5. Golf.
6. *The Book Tower*.
7. Matthew Corbett, son of Harry Corbett.
8. The piano.
9. The St Bernard.

The heaviest dog?

1. Which number cannot be written in Roman numerals?
2. Which creature did Cleopatra use to kill herself?
3. Which food is most popular with Americans when eating out in the USA – pizza, hot dogs or fried chicken?
4. Which superhero is a friend of Lois Lane?
5. In which game might you meet a googly or a chinaman?
6. What sort of woman did Lindsay Wagner play in a TV series?
7. Which American President was nicknamed Ike?
8. Which classical composer wrote the most symphonies?
9. How can you tell the difference between may and hawthorn?

1. The soldiers of which regiment of the British army wear red berets?
2. Who was the first husband of Queen Elizabeth I?
3. Near which city are the Heights of Abraham?
4. Which fictional hero had everything done by Friday?
5. What's the shortest length of time a football league manager has kept his job?
6. How did officials of Gotham City let Batman know he was needed when he didn't answer the Batphone?
7. What sort of job does a pedagogue do?
8. What did my true love send on the first day of Christmas?
9. What's the most important muscle of the human body?

11

1. Nought.
2. An asp, which is a kind of snake.
3. Fried chicken.
4. Superman.
5. Cricket.
6. She played the title role in *The Bionic Woman*.
7. Dwight D. Eisenhower.
8. Haydn (at least 107).
9. You can't – there isn't any difference as these are two names for the same plant.

99

1. The Paratroopers.
2. She never married.
3. Quebec, in Canada.
4. Robinson Crusoe.
5. Three days (by Bill Lampton, at Scunthorpe United).
6. They flashed a silhouette of a bat into the sky.
7. He or she is a teacher.
8. A partridge in a pear tree.
9. The heart.

1. Which word beginning with c describes the skin of well-roasted pork?
2. In which year did Prince Charles marry?
3. Valletta is the capital of which island?
4. What bird did the Cratchits have for their Christmas dinner in *A Christmas Carol* by Dickens?
5. With which sport do you associate Joop Zoetemelk and Laurent Fignon?
6. Which scientist is often imitated because of his habit of flinging his arms about in sweeping gestures?
7. What colour is the Queen's blotting paper?
8. Which musical contains the song 'Don't Cry For Me, Argentina'?
9. Which is the largest living flightless bird?

1. What are the glass reflecting studs down the centre of roads called?
2. In which year did the Russians send their first Sputnik into space?
3. What is the capital of Finland?
4. 'Fee-fi-fo-fum, I smell the blood of . . .' – what?
5. Who has been nicknamed Superbrat?
6. From which island with a grim name did King Kong come?
7. Which comic strip appears in the greatest number of newspapers worldwide?
8. From which film does the song 'Whistle While You Work' come?
9. Which breed of dog does the Queen favour?

12

1. Crackling.
2. It was in 1981.
3. Malta.
4. A goose.
5. Cycling – both have won the Tour de France.
6. Dr Magnus Pyke.
7. It is black so that nobody can read what she has written.
8. *Evita*.
9. The ostrich.

100

1. Cats' eyes.
2. 1957.
3. Helsinki.
4. '. . . an Englishman.'
5. John McEnroe, the tennis player.
6. Skull Island.
7. 'Peanuts'.
8. *Snow White and the Seven Dwarfs*.
9. The corgi.

1. What is the fifteenth letter of the alphabet?
2. Which German ship sank the British battle cruiser, HMS *Hood*?
3. In which country is the world's highest waterfall, Angel Falls?
4. Who is Tom Sawyer's girl friend?
5. With which animal do you associate a matador?
6. Which hero took his girlfriend, Dale Arden, with him when saving the earth from destruction by the planet Mongo?
7. What is the nickname of Alex Higgins, the snooker player?
8. 'New Song', 'What Is Love' and 'Hide and Seek' were the first hits of which popular singer?
9. What is the usual colour of a sapphire?

1. What is the main colour of a £10 note?
2. Which British monarch ruled for 64 years?
3. What's the full name of the OAU, a Third World organization?
4. Who wrote *Black Beauty*?
5. On which river does the annual Oxford *v.* Cambridge boat race take place?
6. What is Terry McCann's job?
7. Of which country was Golda Meir the prime minister?
8. What's the stage name of the folk singer John Deutschendorf, Jr?
9. The Minotaur was half man and half what?

13

1. It is O.
2. The *Bismarck*, in May 1941.
3. Venezuela.
4. Becky Thatcher.
5. The bull.
6. Flash Gordon.
7. He's called Hurricane.
8. Howard Jones.
9. Blue.

101

1. Brown (with a little red).
2. Queen Victoria (actually 63 years, 216 days).
3. Organization of African Unity.
4. Anna Sewell.
5. The Thames.
6. He's a 'minder' (but on his boss's income tax return he's called a gardener!).
7. Israel.
8. John Denver.
9. Bull.

14

1. What kind of work does a stevedore do?
2. What did the Pony Express carry?
3. Where did Charles Lindbergh land when he made the first solo transatlantic flight in 1927?
4. What was the full name of the air ace called Biggles, created by Captain W. E. Johns?
5. How many players make up a rounders side?
6. Who has presented *First Post* and the quiz for teenagers called *Connections*?
7. What's the name of the fat cartoon cat created by Jim Davis?
8. In Dublin's fair city, who died of fever in the song?
9. What do you call carbon dioxide in solid form?

102

1. What does a stitch in time save?
2. Which dictator was sometimes scornfully called Herr Schicklgruber?
3. In which Italian city can you travel by gondola?
4. In which play does Professor Higgins teach Eliza Doolittle to speak properly?
5. In which activity would you use the Fosbury Flop?
6. In which television series did Bill Bixby and Lou Ferrigno both play the central character, depending on how angry he was?
7. How many tiles make up a standard set of dominoes?
8. Which child film star of the 1930s sang about the 'Good Ship Lollipop'?
9. What's the connection between mushrooms and athlete's foot?

14

1. He loads ships in ports or docks.
2. Mail.
3. Paris.
4. James Bigglesworth.
5. Nine.
6. Sue Robbie.
7. Garfield.
8. Sweet Molly Malone.
9. Dry ice.

The Pony Express

102

1. Nine.
2. Adolf Hitler.
3. Venice.
4. *Pygmalion* – which became the musical *My Fair Lady*.
5. High Jumping.
6. *The Incredible Hulk* – Lou was the big green one.
7. Twenty-eight.
8. Shirley Temple.
9. They're both fungi.

1. Which motor-car company made the Silver Ghost?
2. Which famous general was killed at Khartoum in 1885?
3. The city of Phoenix is the capital of which American state?
4. The Artful Dodger appears in which famous novel by Dickens?
5. What nationality is the Wimbledon champion Evonne Cawley?
6. On which eye does Dangermouse wear his patch?
7. Which two colours of paint would you mix to form green?
8. What nickname was given to Gordon Sumner because he wore a black and yellow hooped jersey to a rock band rehearsal?
9. Why does dirty snow melt faster than clean, white snow?

1. What would you do with a Knickerbocker Glory?
2. During which war were the Battles of Crécy and Agincourt fought?
3. In which country can tourists see the Sphinx?
4. In which book does David Pew, the blind beggar, appear?
5. What's the maximum number of rounds fought in a world championship boxing match?
6. Which farm does the Sugden family occupy?
7. What was the surname of the Princess of Wales before she married?
8. Which rock band led by Fish took their name from a Tolkien novel?
9. What's the friendly slang name given to the automatic pilot in an aircraft?

15

1. Rolls-Royce.
2. General Gordon.
3. Arizona.
4. *Oliver Twist.*
5. Australian – she was originally Evonne Goolagong.
6. His left.
7. Blue and yellow.
8. Sting – they thought he looked like a wasp.
9. Dirty snow is darker and darker colours absorb more heat so it melts faster.

103

1. Eat it – it's an ice-cream sundae.
2. The Hundred Years' War.
3. Egypt, near Cairo.
4. *Treasure Island.*
5. Fifteen.
6. Emmerdale Farm, in the Yorkshire TV series.
7. Spencer.
8. Marillion (from *Silmarillion*).
9. George.

1. What would you keep in a bassinet?
2. Who is said to have put his cloak over a muddy patch so that Queen Elizabeth I could cross it with dry feet?
3. Hastings, Romney, Hythe, Dover and Sandwich are called what?
4. In which Shakespeare play do Launcelot Gobbo and Shylock appear?
5. In which sport did Olga Korbut become famous?
6. Kathy Staff plays Doris Luke in which TV series?
7. In the cartoon strip, who owns Snoopy?
8. Which British pop group with a name meaning speedy fashion includes Andy Fletcher and Martin Gore?
9. What's the most common medical complaint in humans?

1. In which occupation would you fly a Jolly Roger?
2. Who was the last British monarch to abdicate?
3. What is the capital of Uganda?
4. In which novel is Heathcliff one of the main characters?
5. Normally a game of table-tennis is played up to how many points?
6. In *The Wizard of Oz*, to which city does the Yellow Brick Road lead?
7. Who's the host of television's *All Star Secrets*?
8. From which film does the Oscar-winning song 'Chim Chim Cheree' come?
9. How many degrees are there in a circle in geometry?

16

1. A baby – it's a sort of cradle.
2. Sir Walter Raleigh.
3. The Cinque Ports.
4. *The Merchant of Venice.*
5. Gymnastics.
6. *Crossroads.*
7. Charlie Brown.
8. Depeche Mode.
9. Back trouble.

104

1. Piracy.
2. Edward VIII, in 1936.
3. Kampala.
4. *Wuthering Heights.*
5. Twenty-one.
6. The Emerald City.
7. Michael Parkinson.
8. *Mary Poppins.*
9. 360.

1. What is the French for thank you?
2. In which year did the Second World War begin?
3. Of which country is Madrid the capital?
4. Which prisoner did Pontius Pilate release instead of Jesus Christ?
5. Which country knocked Britain out of the Davis Cup in 1984?
6. Who created Cosmo Smallpiece?
7. What is the print called that is made from an engraved copper plate?
8. 'Let it Be' was the last song recorded by which group?
9. Vitamins were discovered in 1907. Which was the first?

1. What is *sushi*?
2. Whose last words were, 'I am just going outside and may be some time'?
3. In which sea can't you sink?
4. Rosemary Sutcliff's *The Eagle of the Ninth* is a story about which army's adventures?
5. In which game could a player use a spider?
6. Which 1977 film about the landing of spaceships on Earth was re-released in a special edition in 1980, with added material?
7. For what sort of artistic work was Sir Jacob Epstein famous?
8. Which people invented the bagpipes?
9. Which element forms 27 per cent of the earth's crust?

17

1. Merci.
2. 1939.
3. Spain.
4. Barabbas.
5. Italy.
6. Les Dawson.
7. An etching.
8. The Beatles.
9. Vitamin A – naturally!

105

1. Raw fish – a Japanese delicacy.
2. Lawrence Oates of Captain Scott's South Pole expedition.
3. The Dead Sea.
4. The Roman army in Britain.
5. Snooker – a 'spider' is a tall rest for the cue.
6. *Close Encounters of the Third Kind*.
7. Sculpture.
8. The Greeks – *not* the Scots.
9. Silicon.

1. At what minimum age may you drive a car legally on public roads in Britain?
2. Which stone was the key to the understanding of Egyptian hieroglyphics?
3. Which state in the USA has the largest population?
4. To where would you ride a cock horse?
5. Who stopped Björn Borg from winning Wimbledon for a sixth time?
6. *Gunsmoke* takes place in which city?
7. For what are Lord Snowdon and Patrick Lichfield famous?
8. Who composed the oratorio 'The Creation'?
9. What does a leveret grow up to be?

106

1. Which part of your body should be 'kept to the grindstone' if you are working hard?
2. What was used to keep galley slaves rowing in unison?
3. What is the popular name for the University of Dublin?
4. Which fictional character's friends were Henry, Douglas and Ginger?
5. Which brother and sister team won the Wimbledon mixed doubles title in 1980?
6. Whose horse was Silver?
7. Who painted *The Hay Wain*?
8. Which major key contains no sharps or flats?
9. From which fruit is cider made?

18

1. Seventeen.
2. The Rosetta Stone.
3. California.
4. Banbury Cross.
5. John McEnroe.
6. Dodge City.
7. Photography.
8. Haydn.
9. A hare.

106

1. The nose.
2. A drumbeat.
3. Trinity College.
4. William Brown in the William books.
5. John and Tracy Austin.
6. The Lone Ranger's.
7. John Constable.
8. C major.
9. Apples.

1. Which Common Market member country has a green, white and orange flag?
2. Who preceded Queen Elizabeth II as Britain's monarch?
3. What was the former name of the Baltic port in Poland now called Gdansk?
4. Which Norwegian is called 'the father of modern drama' and wrote *Hedda Gabler*?
5. What do the letters BSA stand for when applied to bikes?
6. Which programme shows the BBC TV International Sheepdog Championship?
7. In which British comic does Dennis the Menace appear?
8. Which pop duo is made up of Alan Barton and Colin Routh?
9. Which tree grows from an acorn?

1. Of what are reef, sheepshank and granny all types?
2. Which king was the first to rule over both England and Scotland?
3. Which US state is called 'the Buckeye State' and has cities called Cincinnati and Toledo?
4. Which Chinese detective was created by Earl Derr Biggers?
5. Who was Britain's heavyweight boxing champion from 1959 to 1969?
6. Which TV series had Kate Jackson, Jaclyn Smith and Farrah Fawcett-Majors as the original three glamorous undercover agents?
7. Which everyday tool did Charles Moncke invent?
8. What was the first musical film ever made?
9. To which family do the wolverine and badger belong?

19

1. Eire.
2. King George VI.
3. Danzig.
4. Henrik Ibsen.
5. Birmingham Small Arms.
6. *One Man and his Dog.*
7. The *Beano.*
8. Black Lace.
9. The oak.

107

One Dog and his Man!

1. They are knots.
2. James VI of Scotland was also James I of England.
3. Ohio.
4. Charlie Chan.
5. Henry Cooper.
6. *Charlie's Angels.*
7. The spanner or monkey wrench.
8. *The Jazz Singer* starring Al Jolson.
9. The weasel family.

1. What are the first two letters of the Greek alphabet?
2. Which mountains did Hannibal cross into Italy to fight the Romans?
3. In which American state are the Everglades?
4. Of what is a bibliomaniac fond?
5. By what name is the team game mintonette now known?
6. What was the occupation of all Seven Dwarfs?
7. Which game is called checkers in the USA?
8. The Attractions back which singer?
9. Which part of your body could suffer from tracheitis or laryngitis?

1. How many hours are there in one week?
2. Prior to being governor of Jamaica, what was Sir Henry Morgan's occupation?
3. By what name are the Cannibal Islands known today?
4. Who wrote the book *Roots*, which became a successful TV series?
5. Who won the Open Golf Championship in 1979 and 1984?
6. In which TV series do the Romulans and the Klingons create problems?
7. Which author who wrote *Tales from Shakespeare* used the pen-name Elia?
8. Which musical contains the song 'Oh, What a Beautiful Morning'?
9. Which plants grow where they're not wanted?

20

1. Alpha, beta.
2. The Alps.
3. Florida.
4. He or she likes books.
5. Volleyball.
6. They were miners.
7. Draughts.
8. Elvis Costello.
9. Your throat.

108

1. 168.
2. He was a pirate.
3. The Fiji Islands.
4. Alex Haley.
5. Severiano Ballesteros.
6. *Star Trek*.
7. Charles Lamb.
8. *Oklahoma*.
9. Weeds.

1. Where would you expect a yokel to live?
2. Which language did the ancient Romans speak?
3. What's the present-day name of Siam, whose capital is Bangkok?
4. In *Charlotte's Web* by E. B. White, what sort of animal is Charlotte the spider's friend, Wilbur?
5. With which sport do you associate Stephen Pickavance, Robin Cousins and John Curry?
6. Which cartoon hero has a friend and sidekick called Penfold?
7. What would you use in the hobby of macramé?
8. Who had hits in 1985 with 'Let's Go Crazy' and '1999'?
9. What would be measured on the Beaufort scale?

1. How many prime numbers are there between ten and twenty?
2. What was the last battle Napoleon ever fought?
3. In which ocean are the islands called the Azores?
4. Which book of the New Testament comes immediately after the four Gospels?
5. Which game is played on the same sort of table as snooker, but uses only three balls?
6. Which programme about hobbies and activities for children was presented by Mick Robertson and Kim Goody?
7. What did Vidal Sassoon do to become famous?
8. Jaz Coleman, Geordie, Raven and Paul make up which pop group?
9. What would be the special study of a palaeontologist, who might want to look around a quarry?

21

1. In the country.
2. Latin.
3. Thailand.
4. A pig.
5. Ice skating.
6. Dangermouse.
7. String, to tie in patterns of knots.
8. Prince.
9. The strength and speed of winds.

109

1. Four: 11, 13, 17, 19.
2. Waterloo in 1815.
3. The Atlantic.
4. The Acts of the Apostles.
5. Billiards.
6. *Freetime*, which ended in March 1985.
7. He is a hairdresser.
8. Killing Joke.
9. Fossils of extinct animals and plants.

1. What sort of food is minestrone?
2. Which English city has had two cathedrals built in it since 1900?
3. If a pilot took off from Paris and flew directly west, what's the first country outside France he would reach?
4. In which famous book can you read about Ben Gunn and Long John Silver?
5. Which football club did Brian Clough manage for more than ten years from 1975 onwards?
6. Which TV police series stars Michael Brandon as an American cop and Glynis Barber as an English lady?
7. Who was the comedian who invented the Diddy Men from Knotty Ash?
8. Who sang with Elaine Paige on their number one hit single 'I Know Him So Well'?
9. What do you call an instrument which measures air pressure?

1. How old do you have to be before you can vote in a British parliamentary election?
2. In which city did a famous 'Tea Party' take place in 1773?
3. Which country has Belgrade as its capital and Serbo-Croat as one of its languages?
4. What is the title of Robert Westall's book about a Newcastle gang of children who steal something from a crashed German plane during the war?
5. In which sport might you do a pike from a tower?
6. Which actor starred in the TV series *Me and My Girl* and *Dick Turpin*?
7. What is the Japanese hobby of *bonsai*, which can be a popular indoor occupation?
8. Which English county has a famous tradition of clog dancing?
9. If you add up all the internal angles of a triangle, what's the total number of degrees?

22

1. Italian soup, with vegetables and pasta.
2. Liverpool.
3. Canada, in Newfoundland.
4. *Treasure Island.*
5. Nottingham Forest.
6. *Dempsey and Makepeace.*
7. Ken Dodd.
8. Barbara Dickson.
9. A barometer.

110

1. Eighteen.
2. Boston, Massachusetts, USA.
3. Yugoslavia.
4. *The Machine Gunners.*
5. Diving.
6. Richard O'Sullivan.
7. Growing very small trees and other plants.
8. Lancashire.
9. 180 degrees.

1. In which country was there a notorious bushranger called Ned Kelly?
2. In which country did the Boxer rebellion take place in the 1890s?
3. Which sea lies between Sweden, Finland and Poland?
4. Who wrote the science fiction stories, *The War of the Worlds*, *The Time Machine* and *The Invisible Man*?
5. In the Olympic Games, which running event will normally take the winner about 2 hours 10 minutes?
6. Which early Saturday morning club for children on TV stars Tommy Boyd, Arabella Warner and James Baker?
7. On which day of the week is the Jewish Sabbath?
8. The last words of which composer were 'I shall hear in heaven'?
9. What does a desalination plant remove from the water that goes into it?

1. What is a pinto?
2. Who was shot by Lee Harvey Oswald in 1963 in Dallas, Texas?
3. From which country do Maoris and kiwis come?
4. What was the name of the hero in a book by Cervantes who charged at windmills, thinking they were giants?
5. In which sport do people compete for the Queen's Prize at Bisley?
6. What's the name of the character played by Mr T on the TV adventure series *The A-Team*?
7. Which famous architect designed the new St Paul's Cathedral after the Great Fire of London?
8. George Michael and Andrew Ridgeley combined to form what?
9. What's the special interest of a horticulturalist?

23

1. Australia.
2. China.
3. The Baltic.
4. H. G. Wells.
5. The marathon.
6. *The Wide-Awake Club*.
7. Saturday.
8. Ludwig van Beethoven.
9. Salt from seawater to make it drinkable.

111

A 'pintomime' horse

1. A piebald horse.
2. President John F. Kennedy.
3. New Zealand.
4. Don Quixote.
5. Rifle-shooting.
6. B. A. Baracus.
7. Sir Christopher Wren.
8. Wham!
9. Growing plants in a garden.

1. Which word can mean both a measuring instrument and a monarch?
2. Who was ruler of England when Guy Fawkes tried to blow up the Houses of Parliament?
3. Which country's flag is blue and white, with a six-pointed star in the centre?
4. Who is the extremely energetic old lady who's the subject of a series of books by Forrest Wilson?
5. In which city is Test cricket played at the Trent Bridge ground?
6. On what subject was the regular television broadcaster Arthur Negus an expert?
7. As what are Sir Michael Hordern and Sir John Gielgud famous?
8. Which composer wrote a famous piano piece called the 'Moonlight Sonata'?
9. What was a Zeppelin, invented by Ferdinand von Zeppelin?

1. Why are labourers sometimes called navvies?
2. Which king of England died at the Battle of Hastings in 1066?
3. How do you spell the name of the continent surrounding the South Pole?
4. Who was the fat monk in Robin Hood's band of men?
5. What does a golfer mean by a divot?
6. With which TV series do you associate Jeremy Beadle, Lee Peck and Martin P. Daniels?
7. What work do people who belong to the trade union called Equity do?
8. The New York High School for the Performing Arts was the setting for which film and TV series?
9. What kind of creature is a Dandie Dinmont?

24

1. Ruler.
2. James I, in 1605.
3. It's Israel's.
4. Supergran.
5. Nottingham.
6. Antiques.
7. Actors.
8. Ludwig van Beethoven.
9. A German airship.

112

1. 'Navvies' is short for 'navigators'; originally they dug canals.
2. Harold.
3. Antarctica, or the Antarctic.
4. Friar Tuck.
5. A lump of earth, hacked out of the ground when hitting a ball.
6. *Game for a Laugh*.
7. They act.
8. *Fame*.
9. A terrier dog.

1. What do you do to a fish when you fillet it?
2. Which general was given Blenheim Palace as a reward for winning the Battle of Blenheim?
3. What is the present-day name of the country once called Persia?
4. Who is the author of the Mister Men books?
5. In which Welsh town is rugby football played at Stradey Park?
6. On which children's TV series does Penelope Keith play Dora, the school bus driver, helped by Ralph McTell?
7. Which famous Englishman's portrait appears on the reverse side of a £20 note?
8. The French composer Saint-Saëns wrote the famous 'Carnival of . . .' – what?
9. The speed of what is measured by an anemometer?

1. What is called the hoosegow or the pen in American slang?
2. Which dictator who ruled Russia had a name meaning 'man of steel'?
3. In which city is there a huge arena called the Colosseum?
4. In the Bible, who murdered his brother Abel?
5. In a tie-breaker in lawn tennis, you must score at least how many points to win the set?
6. What's the name of the 'cool' character played by Henry Winkler in *Happy Days*?
7. Which secretary to the Admiralty wrote a diary that describes the Great Fire of London?
8. To which pop group do Mike Talbot and Paul Weller belong?
9. Which chemical is sometimes added to drinking water to reduce tooth decay?

25

1. Take the bones out.
2. John Churchill, Duke of Marlborough.
3. Iran.
4. Roger Hargreaves.
5. Llanelli.
6. *Tickle on the Tum*.
7. William Shakespeare.
8. 'Carnival of the Animals'.
9. Wind.

113

1. Prison, or 'penitentiary'.
2. Joseph Stalin.
3. Rome.
4. Cain.
5. Seven.
6. Arthur Fonzarelli, or 'the Fonz'.
7. Samuel Pepys.
8. Style Council.
9. Fluoride.

1. Why is a loutish person sometimes called a 'yob'?
2. Which queen of England had seventeen children who all died before she did?
3. If you see the international registration letters CH on the back of a car, which country has it come from?
4. Which hero of Greek myth captured Cerberus, the three-headed dog?
5. With which sport do you associate Ingemar Stenmark, Phil Mahre and Bill Johnson?
6. On which TV panel game do George Gale, Ernie Wise, Barbara Kelly and Patrick Mower appear?
7. What job did the singers Sting, Bryan Ferry, and Tom Bailey of the Thompson Twins all formerly do?
8. Which famous Russian composer wrote the '1812 Overture' in which cannons are fired?
9. Which scientist stated the Theory of Relativity?

1. If an object oscillates, what is it doing?
2. In which battle in Texas in 1836 were Davy Crockett and James Bowie killed?
3. Which famous city's name literally means River of January?
4. In the Bible, how did David kill the giant Goliath?
5. With which sport do you associate Nadia Comaneci and Mary-Lou Retton?
6. What means of transport does Anneka Rice use for the Channel 4 TV quiz *Treasure Hunt*?
7. What were Marco Polo and Leif Ericsson famous for doing?
8. What's the biggest-selling British record of all time, with world sales of over 13 million?
9. What do we call an optical illusion seen by travellers in a desert?

26

1. 'Yob' is backwards slang for boy.
2. Queen Anne.
3. Switzerland.
4. Hercules.
5. Skiing.
6. *What's My Line?*
7. They were teachers.
8. Tchaikovsky.
9. Albert Einstein.

Capturing Cerberus

114

1. It is shaking or vibrating from side to side.
2. The Alamo.
3. Rio de Janeiro, Brazil.
4. With a stone flung from a sling.
5. Gymnastics.
6. Helicopter.
7. Exploring.
8. 'I Want To Hold Your Hand' by the Beatles.
9. A mirage.

1. If someone said, 'Look, there's a juggernaut!', what would you expect to see?
2. Which English king was called *Cœur de Lion* or Lionheart?
3. In which city are the Bronx and Staten Island?
4. Which greedy king of mythology nearly starved because everything he touched turned to gold?
5. How many different numbers are there on a dart board (not counting the bull's-eye or the inner)?
6. What's the name of the small boy who makes friends with the alien visitor in the film *E.T.*?
7. Which black comedian and impressionist became famous on *Three of a Kind*?
8. Which Paul McCartney record spent nine weeks at number one, and sold 2 million copies in Britain?
9. Which creature lies in a nest called a form?

1. What's a cul-de-sac?
2. Which German leader was nicknamed the Iron Chancellor?
3. The Sydney Harbour bridge in Australia is a copy of the bridge in which English city?
4. Which author of *Chitty-Chitty-Bang-Bang* was much better known for creating the character of James Bond?
5. Which world heavyweight champion boxer was nicknamed 'the Brown Bomber'?
6. What's the name of 'superstar' Roland Rat's friend, the gerbil?
7. What were the first names of the classic film comedians Laurel and Hardy?
8. Which record became the biggest-selling album of all time in 1984?
9. Which creature builds a nest called a formicary?

27

1. A large lorry. It might also be a large statue of a god, if you were in India!
2. Richard I.
3. New York.
4. Midas.
5. Twenty.
6. Elliott.
7. Lenny Henry.
8. 'Mull of Kintyre'.
9. A hare.

115

1. A dead-end street.
2. Otto von Bismarck.
3. Newcastle-upon-Tyne.
4. Ian Fleming.
5. Joe Louis.
6. Kevin.
7. Stan and Oliver.
8. 'Thriller' by Michael Jackson.
9. The ant.

1. In the names of the seven days of the week, how many times does the letter D occur?
2. During which war were the Battles of Gettysburg and Bull Run fought?
3. Which country is famous for its fjords?
4. What was Vulcan's job on Mount Olympus?
5. In which sport do the Harlequins, Wasps and Barbarians compete?
6. In which film is Billy Peltzer given a Mogwai he calls Gizmo?
7. What's the name of Princess Anne's husband?
8. In which musical show would you hear the songs 'Climb Every Mountain' and 'The Lonely Goatherd'?
9. What could be operated by a Winchester or a floppy disc?

1. What word is used for hills of sand at the seaside or in deserts?
2. What were Admiral Horatio Nelson's last words at the Battle of Waterloo in 1815?
3. In which European city is there a statue of a little mermaid sitting on a rock?
4. In the Asterix the Gaul books, why do the villagers all hate Cacofonix?
5. Vicarage Road is the home ground of which football team?
6. In *Gremlins*, which cartoon film do all the gremlins visit a cinema to watch?
7. Who's the human who tries to control Emu?
8. Which singer with an elaborately painted face had a big hit in 1982 with 'Goody Two Shoes'?
9. Which scientist invented the modern condensing steam engine in 1765 and first used the term 'horsepower'?

28

1. Eight.
2. The American civil war.
3. Norway.
4. He was the blacksmith of the gods, called Hephaestos by the Greeks.
5. Rugby Union.
6. *Gremlins*.
7. Captain Mark Phillips.
8. *The Sound of Music*.
9. A computer.

116

1. Dunes.
2. He wasn't there – he was killed at Trafalgar, ten years earlier!
3. Copenhagen.
4. He's the bard, and he sings *very* badly!
5. Watford.
6. *Snow White and the Seven Dwarfs*.
7. Rod Hull.
8. Adam, of Adam and the Ants.
9. James Watt.

1. Which colour is called *schwarz* in German and *noir* in French?
2. What were Admiral Horatio Nelson's last words at the Battle of Trafalgar?
3. What is the main town on the Falkland Islands?
4. Who are the tiny people called Pod, Homily and Arrietty, created by Mary Norton?
5. In show jumping, how many penalty points or faults are given for a refusal to jump a fence?
6. What's the name of Postman Pat's cat?
7. What was the surname of the famous engineer whose first names were Isambard Kingdom?
8. How many strings does a classical Spanish guitar have?
9. Some cars have disc brakes; what is the other main type of car brakes?

1. If you dial 999 in an emergency, you have a choice of three main services – what are they?
2. Which social evil did William Wilberforce campaign to abolish?
3. Sarum is the ancient name for which English city?
4. Which book by John Masefield is about Kay Harker, and has the subtitle, *or, When the Wolves were Running*?
5. In which sport did David Wilkie and Duncan Goodhew win Olympic gold medals?
6. With which popular TV series do you associate the characters of Skeletor, Whiplash and Zodac?
7. Which prime minister won the Nobel Prize for Literature?
8. Which song was Paul Young's first big solo hit?
9. What do you call the offspring of a cob and a pen when it hatches out?

29

1. Black.
2. Either, 'Kiss me, Hardy', or 'Kismet, Hardy', meaning, 'It's Fate, Hardy'.
3. Port Stanley.
4. The Borrowers.
5. Three.
6. Jess.
7. Brunel.
8. Six.
9. Drum brakes.

117

1. Police, fire, ambulance – but coastguard as well at the seaside.
2. The slave trade.
3. Salisbury.
4. *The Box of Delights*.
5. Swimming.
6. *He-Man and Masters of the Universe*.
7. Sir Winston Churchill, in 1953.
8. 'Wherever I Lay My Hat'.
9. It's a cygnet or baby swan.

1. If an Australian tells you there's a huge boomer coming, what would you expect to see?
2. Which king ordered that the Domesday Book should be compiled?
3. In which country are Haifa and Tel Aviv?
4. In the Bible, Eve tempted Adam to eat the fruit of which tree?
5. In which indoor sport could you use a paddle in a penholder grip?
6. In which science-fiction film do Paul Atreides, Baron Harkonnen and the Sardaukars appear?
7. If you were going to take up *origami*, what materials would you need?
8. What should a musician do on seeing the word *rallentando* on a piece of music?
9. When sailors suffered from scurvy, which vitamin did they need that fresh fruit could supply?

1. A flotilla is a collection of what?
2. What was the full name of Bonnie Prince Charlie?
3. Around which city was a long and guarded wall built in the 1960s?
4. In the legend, why did the Pied Piper take the children away from Hamelin town?
5. What name is used for a big hole on a golf course filled with sand?
6. In which film would you see Bob Fortuna, Logray, the Ewok Medicine Man, and Sy Snootles and the Rebo Band?
7. Which American President had to use a wheelchair because he was crippled by polio?
8. Which musical team (who wrote *Iolanthe*) broke up when they quarrelled about a carpet?
9. What word is used for a baby whale?

30

1. A large kangaroo.
2. William I – the Conqueror.
3. Israel.
4. The Tree of Knowledge. It's *not* called an apple tree in the Bible.
5. Table-tennis.
6. *Dune.*
7. Pieces of paper, for folding.
8. Slow down.
9. Vitamin C.

118

The bunker

1. Boats.
2. He was Charles Edward Stuart.
3. West Berlin.
4. The Mayor wouldn't pay him for taking away a plague of rats.
5. Bunker.
6. *The Return of the Jedi.*
7. Franklin D. Roosevelt.
8. W. S. Gilbert and Sir Arthur Sullivan.
9. Calf.

1. To how many new pence is the old half-crown equal?
2. Who preceded Hosni Mubarak as President of Egypt?
3. If you were spending kopeks, in which country would you most likely be?
4. Who wrote an autobiography called *Mein Kampf*, or *My Struggle*?
5. Name the Spinks brothers, who both became world boxing champions.
6. In which TV police series do cops called Sonny Crockett and Ricardo Tubbs appear?
7. What is the first name of Prince Charles's second son?
8. On whose life is the show *Evita* based?
9. What is studied in the science of acoustics?

1. How many are in an octet?
2. Which Paris prison was stormed at the start of the French Revolution?
3. Which Danish explorer gave his name to a sea, a strait and an island?
4. Which is the most frequently used letter in the English language?
5. In which sport do you score strikes and spares?
6. What colour is the hair of Batman's enemy, the Joker?
7. What did George Sand and George Eliot have in common?
8. Who is Roxy Music's lead singer?
9. Mercury is a metal, but what does it look like at room temperature?

31

1. 12½p.
2. Anwar Sadat.
3. Russia.
4. Adolf Hitler.
5. Leon and Michael.
6. *Miami Vice*.
7. Henry.
8. Eva Perón's.
9. Sound.

119

1. Eight.
2. The Bastille.
3. Vitus Bering.
4. E.
5. Ten-pin bowling.
6. Green.
7. They were women writers using men's names.
8. Brian Ferry.
9. A silvery liquid.

1. In the nursery rhyme, what disasters did the ladybird face on her return home?
2. Between the armies of which countries was the Battle of Agincourt fought?
3. What is the capital of Poland?
4. In *The Jungle Book* Mowgli is carried off by the Bandar-Log and rescued by Baloo and Baghera. Who are the Bandar-Log?
5. Which sport features in the film *Rocky*?
6. What is the Magnificent Evans's first name in the TV comedy series?
7. How many pockets has a snooker table?
8. Robin and Ali Campbell called their reggae band after the unemployment benefit card – what's its name?
9. On the leaves of which tree do silkworms feed?

1. Which month is said to come in like a lion and go out like a lamb?
2. Which nineteenth-century textile workers smashed up machinery?
3. In 1984 of which country did Laurent Fabius become prime minister?
4. What is the last word of the Bible?
5. How many gold medals did the UK win at the 1984 Summer Olympics?
6. On what sort of TV programme would you expect to see Pamela Armstrong?
7. Which stone animals lie at the base of Nelson's column in Trafalgar Square, London?
8. As what was Sir John Barbirolli renowned?
9. What does a tadpole grow up to be?

32

1. 'Your house is on fire and your children all gone'.
2. England and France.
3. Warsaw.
4. The Monkey-People.
5. Boxing.
6. Plantagenet.
7. Six.
8. UB40.
9. The mulberry.

120

1. March.
2. It was the Luddites, who were scared that unemployment would result from the introduction of machinery.
3. France.
4. Amen.
5. Five.
6. A news programme on ITN.
7. Lions, sculpted by Sir Edwin Landseer.
8. A conductor.
9. A frog.

Duckpole or poleduck?

1. What did Little Red Riding Hood find in her grandmother's bed?
2. Which country was ruled by Catherine de Medici in the sixteenth century?
3. What is the capital of Australia?
4. Which animal-loving doctor was created by Hugh Lofting?
5. From which country does tennis player Rod Laver come?
6. What does 'sitcom' stand for?
7. Which former leader of the House of Lords is the father of Lady Antonia Fraser?
8. Which instrument did Nero play while Rome burned?
9. What are kept in aviaries?

1. How many days are there in November?
2. How many journeys to the New World did Christopher Columbus make?
3. What is the former American city of New Amsterdam now called?
4. Who wrote the long poem *The Faerie Queene* in 1579?
5. Which later world heavyweight boxing champion from Sweden was disqualified for not trying in the 1952 Olympics?
6. Who played Fanny Brice in *Funny Girl* and *Funny Lady*?
7. Who was the first American president born in the twentieth century?
8. In *The Sound of Music*, which alpine flower is featured in song?
9. Why does a jumping bean jump?

33

1. The wolf.
2. France – she was the wife of Henry II.
3. Canberra.
4. Dr Dolittle.
5. Australia.
6. Situation comedy.
7. Lord Longford.
8. The lyre (the fiddle hadn't been invented).
9. Birds.

Nero's Disco Inferno!

121

1. Thirty.
2. Four.
3. New York.
4. Edmund Spenser.
5. Ingemar Johansson.
6. Barbra Streisand.
7. John F. Kennedy, who was born on 29 May 1917.
8. The edelweiss.
9. Because a moth larva, born inside the bean, moves about.

1. What number does the Roman numeral C represent?
2. Who first flew the Atlantic in 1919 with Arthur Brown?
3. Which London Row is particularly associated with tailoring?
4. Which poet wrote the 'play for voices' called *Under Milk Wood*?
5. For which football league side did Martin Peters, Bobby Moore and Geoff Hurst all play?
6. For what is Telly Savalas's first name short?
7. Name two of the four US presidents whose faces are carved on Mount Rushmore.
8. On which Dickens novel was the musical *Oliver* based?
9. Which creature is the only mammal to have a shell?

1. Which sign of the zodiac is represented by a bull?
2. In which year in Britain did the wearing of seat belts in the front seats of cars become compulsory?
3. Which Irish port is at the head of the Shannon estuary?
4. How many lines form a limerick?
5. How long does a single round last in professional boxing?
6. Who stars as the policeman in *Beverly Hills Cop*, the comedy film?
7. Which chess piece is the most mobile?
8. Who wrote the opera *Rigoletto*?
9. What is a cow called before it has given birth to a calf?

34

1. 100.
2. John Alcock.
3. Savile Row.
4. Dylan Thomas.
5. West Ham.
6. Aristotle.
7. George Washington, Thomas Jefferson, Abraham Lincoln, Theodore Roosevelt.
8. *Oliver Twist*.
9. The armadillo.

122

1. Taurus.
2. 1983.
3. Limerick.
4. Five (long, long, short, short, long).
5. Three minutes.
6. Eddie Murphy.
7. The queen.
8. Giuseppe Verdi – which is the Italian for Joe Green.
9. A heifer.

1. What sort of ship is designed to carry very large liquid cargoes?
2. Which civil war was fought between 1936 and 1939?
3. Of where is Desmond Tutu the bishop?
4. Porthos, Aramis – which is the missing Musketeer?
5. What nationality was Rosie Ackermann, the first woman to high-jump 2 metres?
6. What's the BBC's regular early-morning TV programme called?
7. Ferdy and Morty are nephews of which cartoon character?
8. Kiki Dee had a hit with 'Don't Go Breaking My Heart', sung with whom?
9. How many degrees are in a right angle?

1. Three score years and ten – if you'd lived this long, how old would you be?
2. Where was Sir Walter Raleigh executed?
3. What is one-hundredth of a German mark?
4. Into what did the Ugly Duckling turn?
5. Does squash, tennis, golf or table-tennis use the largest ball?
6. How many Dalmatians were there in the Walt Disney film?
7. In 1985 the colour television licence fee went up from £46 – to what?
8. In which opera does Mimi feature?
9. What was the first orbiting space laboratory, launched in 1973?

35

1. A tanker, or VLCC – Very Large Crude Carrier.
2. The Spanish civil war.
3. Johannesburg. Bishop Tutu won the Nobel Peace Prize in 1984.
4. Athos – D'Artagnan joined later.
5. East German.
6. *Breakfast Time*.
7. Mickey Mouse.
8. Elton John.
9. 90 degrees.

123

1. Seventy.
2. The Tower of London.
3. One pfennig.
4. A swan.
5. Tennis.
6. 101.
7. £58.
8. *La Bohème*.
9. It was Skylab; it crashed back to earth in 1979.

1. Gules is the heraldic term for which colour?
2. As what did Prince Siddhartha Gautama, who died in 483 BC, become known?
3. What was the name of Ho Chi Minh City prior to 1975?
4. How many sisters had Cinderella?
5. Who beat Everton 1–0 in the 1984 Milk Cup final?
6. In the film of that name, what was Jaws?
7. What do people who call themselves gricers specialize in spotting?
8. How many men are in the pop group Bananarama?
9. Where in Europe does a small colony of tailless Barbary apes live (not in a zoo)?

1. What is the French word for three?
2. Which motoring organization was founded in 1905?
3. In which country are some policemen called *gendarmes*?
4. In Greek legend, who supported the world on his shoulders?
5. Who beat Sunderland 1–0 in the 1985 Milk Cup final?
6. In which TV police series does Anna Carteret play Inspector Kate Longton?
7. Antony Armstrong-Jones was given what title?
8. Which pop group is named after the bowler-hatted detectives in Herge's 'Tintin' cartoons?
9. Upon what does the baobab tree in Africa depend for pollination?

36

1. Red.
2. Buddha.
3. Saigon.
4. Two, both ugly.
5. Liverpool.
6. A great white shark.
7. Trains.
8. None – the group are all female.
9. On the Rock of Gibraltar.

124

1. *Trois*.
2. The AA, or Automobile Association.
3. France.
4. Atlas, after whom the books of maps were named.
5. Norwich.
6. *Juliet Bravo* – the title is her radio call sign.
7. He became the Earl of Snowdon.
8. The Thompson Twins.
9. Bats.

1. In an American university, during which year is a student called a sophomore?
2. Which English king, called 'the Great', died in 899?
3. Which South American country named after a wet part of Italy was discovered by Alonso de Ojeda?
4. Which Gospel writer in the Bible was a tax-collector?
5. Who, in 1979, created a new record by winning her twentieth Wimbledon title?
6. Which city suburb is considered to be the film capital of the world?
7. Which famous novelist is the Princess of Wales's step-grandmother?
8. Which piece of music did Handel compose especially for George I?
9. Which sea creature has a beak like a parrot, eight arms, two tentacles around its mouth and squirts clouds of ink?

1. How many engines powered Charles Lindbergh's plane on his first solo Atlantic crossing?
2. Which English queen first used a flush WC?
3. Which is the country directly west of Egypt in which Benghazi is situated?
4. For how many pieces of silver was Joseph sold into slavery?
5. Who was the first jockey to be knighted?
6. Who stars as Jim Rockford in the TV detective series *The Rockford Files*?
7. For what is Sir Geraint Evans famous?
8. What instrument does the Indian musician Ravi Shankar play?
9. Which part of a flower makes pollen?

37

1. In the second – first-year students are called freshmen.
2. Alfred.
3. Venezuela (named after Venice).
4. Matthew.
5. Billie-Jean King.
6. Hollywood – which is part of Los Angeles.
7. Barbara Cartland, writer of romances.
8. 'The Water Music'.
9. The cuttlefish.

The cuttlefish?

125

1. One – and his journey took him nearly a day and a half!
2. Elizabeth I.
3. Libya.
4. Twenty.
5. Sir Gordon Richards, who was nicknamed 'the shortest knight of the year'.
6. James Garner.
7. As an opera singer, now retired.
8. The sitar.
9. Stamen.

1. What is the qualification for being Father of the House of Commons?
2. Which was England's first university?
3. The capitals of the Seychelles, Hong Kong and British Columbia all have the same name – what is it?
4. Which day of the week is named after the Norse god of war and thunder?
5. Octopush is a new form of hockey. Where is it played?
6. After which city was Rigsby's cat in *Rising Damp* named?
7. Who first won the World Snooker Championship in 1981?
8. Which instrument did Andrés Segovia play?
9. What does a fawn grow up to be?

1. Of what are railway tracks now made?
2. Who was the first Pope?
3. Which country has the world's largest population?
4. Which foods eaten early in the day are named after the Roman goddess of agriculture?
5. How many barriers do runners leap in the seven laps of the Olympic steeplechase?
6. Which actors play the Harts in TV's *Hart to Hart*?
7. Which American comedian's real name is Allen Stewart Konigsberg?
8. How many semiquavers make one crotchet?
9. From what are pearls obtained?

38

1. Being the longest serving Member of Parliament.
2. Oxford, founded about 1167.
3. Victoria.
4. Thursday, after Thor.
5. Along the bottom of a swimming-pool, underwater.
6. Vienna.
7. Steve Davis.
8. The guitar.
9. A deer.

126

1. Steel.
2. St Peter, one of the twelve disciples.
3. China.
4. Cereals, after Ceres.
5. Thirty-five (five in each lap) in 3,000 metres.
6. Stephanie Powers and Robert Wagner.
7. Woody Allen.
8. Four.
9. Oysters and mussels.

1. What's the maximum number of dots or dashes used for any letter in Morse code?
2. Whose tomb did Lord Carnarvon and Howard Carter discover?
3. Which of the United States is nicknamed the Empire State?
4. Who turned Odysseus' men into swine?
5. In which sport do competitors wear mesh visors and white canvas clothes?
6. In which TV comedy series did Frances de la Tour play Miss Jones?
7. How many cards are there in the game of Continuo?
8. What is the more popular name for Mendelssohn's 'Hebrides Overture'?
9. Which other planet is nearest in size to the earth?

1. William Glass founded the guide to the buying and selling of what?
2. The Rainhill Trials of 1829 were held to find out what?
3. Spain and France are separated by which range of mountains?
4. Who wrote the book *The Kon-Tiki Expedition*?
5. Who was the last New Zealand athlete to hold the world record for the mile, set in 1975?
6. Which Marx brother never spoke in their films and was really called Adolph?
7. Sage is a shade of which colour?
8. How many bags of wool did the black sheep have?
9. Which mammal lays eggs, has webbed feet, a duck's bill, and poisonous spurs on its hind legs?

39

1. Four.
2. Tutankhamun's.
3. New York.
4. Circe.
5. Fencing.
6. *Rising Damp*.
7. Forty-two.
8. 'Fingal's Cave'.
9. Venus, which is slightly smaller.

127

1. Used cars.
2. The best locomotive – Stephenson's 'Rocket' won.
3. The Pyrenees.
4. Thor Heyerdahl.
5. John Walker.
6. Harpo.
7. Green.
8. Three.
9. The duckbilled platypus.

1. Over what did the cow jump in the nursery rhyme?
2. What was Queen Victoria's title in India?
3. In which country might you live on a kibbutz?
4. Which is the last book of the Old Testament?
5. What colour jersey does the leader in cycling stage-races wear?
6. Who is Bamm-Bamm's father in the cartoon series *The Flintstones*?
7. Which great artist painted 'The Last Supper'?
8. Which is the lowest voice – soprano, contralto or mezzo-soprano?
9. Which animal has the same name as one of the Deadly Sins?

1. What word describes both a type of shoe and an Irish accent?
2. Which was the first mass-produced British car?
3. In which country is the Great Bear lake?
4. Which is the fourth book of the Old Testament?
5. FIFA is the governing body of which sport?
6. In which TV series did Clint Eastwood play Rowdy Yates?
7. Who first demonstrated TV in public?
8. Flutes and recorders are played differently – what's the difference?
9. What does a foal grow up to be?

40

1. The moon.
2. Empress of India.
3. Israel.
4. Malachi.
5. Yellow.
6. Barney Rubble.
7. Leonardo da Vinci.
8. Contralto.
9. The sloth.

Who sings the lowest?

128

1. Brogue.
2. The Austin Seven.
3. Canada.
4. Numbers.
5. Soccer.
6. *Rawhide*.
7. John Logie Baird.
8. You blow across a hole in a flute, and down into a hole in a recorder.
9. A horse or pony.

41

1. Why do Australians never expect snow at Christmas?
2. Who became Lord Protector of England in 1653?
3. England's smallest county used to be Rutland, but that's now been made a part of which larger county?
4. What kind of animal is Tarka in Henry Williamson's book?
5. In lawn tennis, how many championships make up the Grand Slam?
6. In *The A-Team*, what job does Murdock do?
7. What title did Mrs Bessie Wallis Simpson take in 1937 when she married the former King Edward VIII?
8. Which band from Coventry had their first big hit with 'Love and Pride'?
9. Which British surgeon first used carbolic acid as an antiseptic in operations?

129

1. What do the letters mpg represent in cars?
2. Which British king ruled for sixty years, though not quite as long as Queen Victoria?
3. When people go to the Algarve on holiday, which country do they visit?
4. What's the home of the gods in Norse mythology called?
5. With which sport do you associate Michael Whitaker, John Whitaker and Nick Skelton?
6. In which TV series would you see little creatures called Doozers, who just *love* to work?
7. Which game played with dice and counters has a Latin name meaning, I play?
8. Which singer persuaded Neil Kinnock to appear in her video of 'My Guy'?
9. What is the name of the amount of energy needed to raise the temperature of a gram of water by 1 degree centigrade?

41

1. Because December is midsummer in the southern hemisphere.
2. Oliver Cromwell.
3. Leicestershire.
4. An otter.
5. Four: those played at Wimbledon, and in the USA, France and Australia.
6. He's the pilot.
7. She became the Duchess of Windsor.
8. King.
9. Joseph Lister.

129

1. Miles per gallon.
2. George III, 1760–1820.
3. Portugal.
4. Valhalla.
5. Show jumping.
6. *Fraggle Rock*.
7. Ludo.
8. Tracey Ullman.
9. Calorie.

1. What are called *pommes de terre*, or 'earth apples', in French?
2. What were joined in Britain by the Act of Union of 1707?
3. Which two seas are connected by the Suez Canal?
4. *The Sword in the Stone* tells the story of young Wart, who grew up to be . . . who?
5. Which sport do Pam Shriver and Peanut Louie play?
6. In which long-running TV serial are Henry Wilks and Amos Brearly characters?
7. For what are Wayne Sleep and Bonnie Langford famous?
8. Who sang the title song from the 1985 magical film *The Neverending Story*?
9. What did Alfred Nobel invent that made him enough money to found the Nobel Prizes?

1. How many blocks 2 centimetres square could you fit into a space 8 centimetres by 6 centimetres?
2. Who is the only American president this century never to have been elected either president or vice-president?
3. Of which country is Reykjavik the capital?
4. Who wrote books about Thursday the mouse and the guinea-pig Olga de Polga?
5. How much have you scored in darts if you hit double-top twice?
6. Who plays Paul Michael Glaser's partner in *Starsky and Hutch*?
7. Which comedian whose real name is Maurice Cole created the characters of Sid Snot and Captain Kremmen?
8. Which pop group contains Annie Lennox and Dave Stewart?
9. What's the largest meat-eating animal living in Britain, apart from in zoos?

42

1. Potatoes.
2. England and Scotland.
3. The Mediterranean Sea and the Red Sea.
4. King Arthur.
5. Lawn tennis.
6. *Emmerdale Farm*.
7. Dancing.
8. Limahl.
9. Dynamite.

130

1. Twelve.
2. Gerald Ford.
3. Iceland.
4. Michael Bond.
5. Eighty.
6. David Soul.
7. Kenny Everett.
8. Eurythmics.
9. Man! The largest *wild* carnivore is the badger.

1. Which plant provides the main food of the giant panda?
2. Which dictator of Italy was assassinated in 1945 and hanged upside down?
3. Which stretch of water do you cross to get from Southampton to the Isle of Wight?
4. Which fictional character is called the Saint?
5. What was Captain Matthew Webb the first man to accomplish?
6. In *Supergran* who sings the title song?
7. From which country does Dame Edna Everage (played by Barrie Humphries) come?
8. Which TV pop music programme has Zoë Brown and Alastair Pirie as presenters?
9. What sort of camel has two humps?

1. What do we usually call St Stephen's Day?
2. The Ottoman Empire was based on which country?
3. When sailors talk about going to Pompey, which port do they mean?
4. Who's the old miser who reforms in Dickens's *A Christmas Carol*?
5. How many players are there in an American football side, not counting substitutes?
6. In which puppet programme could you see the evil Queen Zelda?
7. What was the surname of Sir John, who until his death in 1984 was poet laureate?
8. Which comedy music group is made up of Graham, Maurice, Carl, Robin and Albert?
9. Which scientist put forward his theory of evolution in *On the Origin of Species*?

43

1. Bamboo.
2. Benito Mussolini.
3. The Solent.
4. Simon Templar.
5. Swimming the English Channel.
6. Billy Connolly.
7. Australia.
8. *Razzmatazz*.
9. The Bactrian.

131

1. Boxing Day.
2. Turkey.
3. Portsmouth.
4. Ebenezer Scrooge.
5. Eleven.
6. *Terrahawks*.
7. Betjeman.
8. The Grumbleweeds.
9. Charles Darwin.

1. Who would use a metronome, and what for?
2. Which president of the USA (the thirty-third) had a name meaning ironworker in German?
3. The capital city of Brazil used to be Rio de Janeiro. What is it now?
4. Who wrote the books in which Ruth Blackett is called Nancy because pirates should be ruthless, and she'd like to be a pirate?
5. In which indoor sport could you do a fliffus, knee-drop or barani-in?
6. Which British actor played Inspector Clouseau in the Pink Panther films?
7. Which singer is closely connected with Watford Football Club?
8. What's the title of Channel 4's pop-music programme presented by Jools Holland and Paula Yates?
9. The coloured circle around the pupil of your eye is called what?

1. In what industry were Davy lamps once used?
2. In olden days, people were expected to give tithes to the Church. What was a tithe?
3. The USA has four states whose names begin with W. Washington is one; can you name one of the other three?
4. Who runs the huge chocolate factory that Charlie Bucket and four other children visit in Roald Dahl's book?
5. Which sport on TV do Brough Scott, Lord Oaksey and Peter O'Sullevan describe?
6. Which film was the sequel to *Raiders of the Lost Ark*?
7. Who digs in the ground to find evidence of past civilizations?
8. Which male pop singer co-starred with Diana Ross in *The Wiz*?
9. From which chemical element is a diamond formed?

44

1. A musician, for beating time regularly.
2. Dwight D. Eisenhower.
3. Brasilia.
4. Arthur Ransome – *Swallows and Amazons* and other titles.
5. Trampolining.
6. Peter Sellers.
7. Elton John.
8. *The Tube*.
9. The iris.

132

1. Mining.
2. One-tenth of your income, a sort of tax.
3. Wyoming, Wisconsin, and West Virginia.
4. Willie Wonka.
5. Horse racing.
6. *Indiana Jones and the Temple of Doom*.
7. An archaeologist.
8. Michael Jackson – he played the Scarecrow.
9. Carbon.

1. In the proverb, what do many hands do?
2. Which travelling preacher started the Methodist religious movement?
3. What's the capital of Turkey?
4. Which writer who has become poet laureate wrote *The Iron Man* and *Meet My Folks*?
5. For which sport did Malcolm Cooper win a gold medal for Britain in the 1984 Olympics, scoring 1173 points?
6. Which film followed *Star Wars* and *The Empire Strikes Back*?
7. After which American president was the teddy bear named?
8. In music the word *forte* means loudly – which word means quietly?
9. Only one planet in our solar system has just two moons, called Phobos and Deimos. Which planet?

1. From the leaves of which tree is the wreath made, traditionally, that is given to the winner of a sporting event?
2. Which queen of France was guillotined during the French Revolution?
3. Which river is sacred to the Hindu religion?
4. Who wrote about Mrs Tiggy-Winkle, Jeremy Fisher and Pigling Bland?
5. If in darts you need twenty to finish but hit a six by mistake, which double should you aim at next?
6. Which comedian's TV show is a 'Madhouse'?
7. What might you visit at Chessington or Whipsnade?
8. What does the instruction *da capo* mean on a piece of music?
9. Which Greek mathematician's name is given to the theorem about the squares on the three sides of a right-angled triangle?

45

1. Make light work.
2. John Wesley (1703–91).
3. Ankara, *not* Istanbul as many people think!
4. Ted Hughes.
5. Rifle-shooting.
6. *The Return of the Jedi*.
7. Theodore Roosevelt.
8. *Piano*.
9. Mars.

133

The all-American bear?

1. Laurel.
2. Marie-Antoinette.
3. The Ganges.
4. Beatrix Potter.
5. Double seven.
6. Russ Abbot.
7. A zoo.
8. Go back to the beginning and start again.
9. Pythagoras – but he didn't invent it as it was known by the ancient Egyptians.

1. What should a person who has claustrophobia try to avoid?
2. What did the Lancastrians use as their badge when they fought the Yorkists from 1455 to 1485?
3. What language do the people of Austria speak?
4. If an adverb describes a verb, what describes a noun?
5. In which sport do people compete for the Federation Cup, the Wightman Cup and the King's Cup?
6. Which great actor played Ben Obi-Wan Kenobi in *Star Wars*?
7. Which comedian used to be the partner of Ernie Wise?
8. What's the surname of Andy, Roger and John, three members of Duran Duran?
9. Where in your body are your incisors and your canines?

1. Which organization would own a van with PDSA painted on its side?
2. Which general invaded Britain in the year 55 BC?
3. The capital city of which country stands on the River Vistula?
4. Who had a coat of many colours in the Bible?
5. In which year were the Olympic Games last held in London (the year Prince Charles was born)?
6. Which cookery expert from TV-AM became in 1985 a presenter of *Game for a Laugh*?
7. To which political party do Mr Cyril Smith and Mr David Steel belong?
8. Which famous series of concerts was begun by Sir Henry Wood?
9. How many minutes does it take light to travel from the sun to the earth?

46

1. Being shut in enclosed spaces.
2. The red rose – the Yorkists used the white rose.
3. German.
4. An adjective.
5. Lawn tennis.
6. Sir Alec Guinness.
7. Eric Morecambe.
8. Taylor.
9. Jaw or mouth – they're teeth.

134

1. People's Dispensary for Sick Animals.
2. Julius Caesar.
3. Poland – it's Warsaw.
4. Joseph.
5. 1948.
6. Rustie Lee.
7. Liberals.
8. The Promenade Concerts or Proms.
9. About eight to eight and a half, but it *is* downhill all the way!

1. What sort of work does a 'chippy' do?
2. Which king is said to have shouted, 'A horse, a horse, my kingdom for a horse!'?
3. Which city was the Italian artist Canaletto most famous for painting – and there is a clue in his name?
4. On what topic did Mrs Beeton and Elizabeth David write books?
5. What is special about a boxer called a southpaw?
6. Who followed Peter Davison as Doctor Who?
7. Who has his summer home at Castel Gandolfo, not far from Rome?
8. To which group with a number in its name did Nick Heyward belong?
9. 'Richard Of York Gained Battles In Vain' helps you to remember what?

1. What is the maximum number of great-grandparents any person may have?
2. Who was the first Prime Minister of England?
3. In which country is the Zuider Zee?
4. Who wrote *Vanity Fair* and had Makepeace as his middle name?
5. In which sport might you see Carl Prean play Desmond Douglas?
6. On which two days of the week is 'Blue Peter' normally shown?
7. What is particularly remarkable about the appearance of Mr Spock in *Star Trek*?
8. Which singer was with the Rich Kids and Slik before joining Ultravox?
9. What collective name do you give to a group of lions?

47

1. 'Chippy' is a nickname for a carpenter who works with wood.
2. Richard III, killed at the Battle of Bosworth.
3. Venice.
4. Cookery.
5. He is left-handed.
6. Colin Baker.
7. The Pope.
8. Haircut 100.
9. The colours of the rainbow in order – Red, Orange, Yellow, Green, Blue, Indigo, Violet.

'A horse, a horse, my kingdom for a horse!'

135

1. Eight.
2. Sir Robert Walpole.
3. Holland, or the Netherlands.
4. William Makepeace Thackeray.
5. Table-tennis.
6. Monday and Thursday.
7. He has pointed ears.
8. Midge Ure.
9. A pride.

1. In a book, what does a small letter c with a circle around it mean?
2. Who led the Free French in the Second World War and later became president of France?
3. Which country has a name meaning silver?
4. Who wrote the science fiction stories *Chocky* and *The Day of the Triffids*?
5. How far is the penalty spot from the goal line in soccer?
6. In which Eastern country is the musical film *The King and I* set?
7. If someone offered to try acupuncture on you, what would you expect them to do?
8. What does a musician use to play a xylophone?
9. What name is used for a portable hut or building and also for a kind of tortoise?

1. What do the letters RIP on a gravestone mean?
2. If you add together the number of British monarchs called Henry and those called George, what's the total?
3. What's the main unit of currency used in Switzerland?
4. Which artist has produced *Haunted House* and illustrated the Meg and Mog books?
5. In which sport might you see a caddie with a niblick?
6. Who took over from Bob Monkhouse as host of the TV game show *Family Fortunes*?
7. Who is the head of the Church of England?
8. Which seven-member pop group, including Suggs, had a number one hit called 'House of Fun'?
9. Where would you find a Van Allen belt?

48

1. Copyright.
2. General Charles de Gaulle.
3. Argentina.
4. John Wyndham.
5. 12 yards or 11 metres.
6. Siam, or Thailand.
7. Stick pins in you to cure aches and pains.
8. Hammers, to hit the bars of the instrument.
9. Terrapin.

136

1. Rest in peace, or *requiescat in pace* in Latin.
2. Fourteen – eight Henrys plus six Georges.
3. Swiss franc.
4. Jan Pienkowski.
5. Golf.
6. Max Bygraves.
7. The Queen. The Archbishop of Canterbury comes next.
8. Madness.
9. In the sky – it's a layer of radiation high above the earth.

1. From which nuts is marzipan made?
2. Which king of England is best remembered for unsuccessfully ordering the tide not to come in?
3. The capital of the USA is called in full Washington, DC. What does DC mean?
4. What nickname did Sir Percy Blakeney use in the stories where he saved aristocrats from the French Revolution?
5. In which sport do players hit a shuttlecock?
6. In the film *Mary Poppins* what is Mary Poppins's job?
7. Of which country was Pierre Trudeau once the prime minister?
8. Cello, viola, bassoon, double bass – which of these instruments is not played with a bow?
9. What is Mach 3?

1. What does a vintner do?
2. When France was part of the Roman Empire, what was its Latin name?
3. A car with E as its international registration letter comes from which country?
4. What was the surname of the three novelist sisters Emily, Anne and Charlotte?
5. With which game do you associate Nigel Short and Anatoly Karpov?
6. Which job is done by Donald Turner, hero of the TV series *One by One*?
7. For what sort of hobby would someone use an SLR?
8. The British star group that made the record 'Do They Know It's Christmas?' was called Band Aid. What was the name of the American star group that made 'We Are the World'?
9. If a meat-eating animal is a carnivore, what's a plant-eating animal called?

49

1. Almonds.
2. Canute.
3. District of Columbia.
4. The Scarlet Pimpernel.
5. Badminton.
6. She's the nanny.
7. Canada.
8. Bassoon.
9. Three times the speed of sound.

Tongue-tide?

137

1. Sells wines and spirits.
2. Gaul, or Gallia.
3. Spain – España.
4. Brontë.
5. Chess.
6. Veterinary surgeon at a zoo.
7. Photography – it's a Single Lens Reflex camera.
8. USA for Africa.
9. A herbivore.

1. Which one word means 'a person 100 years old'?
2. Which king who ruled from 1272 to 1307 had eighteen children?
3. Which language do the people of Brazil speak?
4. What is James Bond's agent number?
5. Where in France is a 24-hour motor race held annually?
6. What are the surnames of Sid and Eddie in the TV comedy team?
7. Why does Robert Pershing Wadlow, who died in 1940, have his name and picture in *The Guinness Book of Records*?
8. 'Do You Really Want To Hurt Me?' was the first number one record for which group?
9. What was the name of the lioness in *Born Free* and *Living Free*?

1. What does a modern sailor mean when he refers to the galley?
2. What do we call the huge ships that sailed with the Spanish Armada?
3. In which state of the USA are Houston, Dallas and Fort Worth?
4. Which month is named after the Roman god of war?
5. What does a golfer mean by the 'nineteenth hole'?
6. In which war was the TV serial *By the Sword Divided* set?
7. What's the main ingredient of a dish from Switzerland called *fondue*?
8. Which film musical contained the songs 'You're The One That I Want' and 'Summer Nights'?
9. Which month of the year contains the longest day?

50

1. Centenarian.
2. Edward I.
3. Portuguese.
4. 007.
5. Le Mans.
6. Little and Large.
7. He was the tallest provable giant – 272 centimetres or 8 feet 11 inches tall.
8. Culture Club.
9. Elsa.

138

1. The ship's kitchen.
2. Galleons.
3. Texas.
4. March, after Mars.
5. The golf-course clubhouse or the bar.
6. The English Civil War.
7. Melted cheese.
8. *Grease*.
9. June – it's the 21st.

1. What is done with clocks and watches when British Summer Time begins?
2. On which island did the unsuccessful Bay of Pigs invasion take place in 1961?
3. In which country is Orly Airport?
4. Who was Winnie-the-Pooh's donkey friend?
5. What was the real first name of champion boxer, Sonny Liston?
6. Who was the Oscar-winning star of the film *Ben Hur*?
7. Whom did Robin Hood marry?
8. In which section of an orchestra would you find a bassoon?
9. How many tentacles has an octopus?

1. What's the British term for what Americans call faucets?
2. Which has been the most common first name of American presidents?
3. Which English holiday resort is near Beachy Head?
4. What was the name of King Arthur's magic sword?
5. With which sport is Sunningdale connected?
6. In which TV programme might you visit the Queen Vic or Al's Café?
7. In a rainbow red is at one end of the spectrum. Which colour is at the other?
8. Which dance was banned in Paris in the nineteenth century?
9. What sort of creature is a capybara?

51

1. They are put forward one hour.
2. Cuba.
3. France, near Paris.
4. Eeyore.
5. Charles.
6. Charlton Heston.
7. Maid Marian.
8. Woodwind section.
9. Eight.

139

1. Taps for water.
2. James.
3. Eastbourne.
4. Excalibur.
5. Golf.
6. *EastEnders*.
7. Violet.
8. The can-can.
9. A very large rodent.

1. What is a balalaika?
2. Which ship, sunk in the reign of Henry VIII, was raised in 1982?
3. Which is the world's highest mountain?
4. What sort of beast may a lycanthrope turn into when there's a full moon?
5. Which soccer team plays home matches at Highbury?
6. In commercial TV and radio, for what do the letters IBA stand?
7. Whose autobiography is called *And This Is Me*?
8. Who had a number one hit with 'A Little Peace' after winning the Eurovision Song Contest?
9. What are the five senses?

1. How many men did the Duke of York march up and down the hill?
2. The Earl of Wilmington and Henry Pelham were the second and third men to be what?
3. Of which country is Stockholm the capital?
4. Who is 'a bear of very little brain' in a famous children's book?
5. Which indoor game took its name from an English country house?
6. Which actor starred as Jack Regan in *The Sweeney*, then as the ace reporter in *Mitch*?
7. 'It's the way I tell 'em!' is the catch-phrase of which Irish comedian?
8. Which group had a number one hit with 'Don't You Want Me?'?
9. For what is H_2O the chemical symbol?

52

1. A musical instrument from Russia.
2. The *Mary Rose*.
3. Mount Everest.
4. A wolf – a lycanthrope is a werewolf.
5. Arsenal.
6. Independent Broadcasting Authority.
7. Mike Yarwood.
8. Nicole.
9. Sound, sight, taste, smell and touch.

140

1. 10,000.
2. Prime minister – the first was Robert Walpole.
3. Sweden.
4. Winnie-the-Pooh.
5. Badminton.
6. John Thaw.
7. Frank Carson.
8. Human League.
9. A molecule of water.

1. For what is Ltd the abbreviation?
2. Between which two armies was the Battle of Bannockburn fought?
3. In which country would you spend forints?
4. Who went to sea in 'a beautiful pea-green boat'?
5. Which is the longest race at the Olympic Games?
6. What's the name of the public house in *Coronation Street*?
7. Who robbed the rich to give to the poor around Nottingham?
8. Who wear tutus when working?
9. Is aquamarine normally red, blue, green or yellow?

1. On which value of bank note does a picture of Sir Christopher Wren appear?
2. Which is the oldest of the seven wonders of the world?
3. Which is the largest lake in Africa?
4. Who led the Israelites out of Egypt?
5. On which racecourse is the Prix de l'Arc de Triomphe run?
6. In which TV series have Arnold and Willis Jackson been adopted by a wealthy family?
7. What does a thespian do?
8. Brass, woodwind, percussion – what's the missing fourth section of a symphony orchestra?
9. How many pints make 1 gallon?

53

1. Limited.
2. The English and the Scots.
3. Hungary.
4. The owl and the pussycat.
5. The cycling road-race – about 200 kilometres.
6. The Rovers Return.
7. Robin Hood.
8. Female ballet dancers.
9. Blue.

141

1. On the £50-note – have a look through your pocket money!
2. The pyramids of Egypt.
3. Lake Victoria.
4. Moses.
5. Longchamps.
6. *Diff'rent Strokes*.
7. Acts – it is a posh word for an actor.
8. Strings.
9. Eight.

1. What is the registration number of the Queen's official cars?
2. What preceded the hot-water bottle for taking the chill off beds?
3. Which US state is nicknamed 'Land of the Midnight Sun' and 'the Last Frontier'?
4. Which word completes the book title, *The Swiss Family* . . . ?
5. If you were at cover point or square leg, what game would you be playing?
6. What is the longest-running radio serial in Britain?
7. Whose horse was Black Bess?
8. Which is the largest instrument in the strings section of an orchestra?
9. From which animal does mutton come?

1. Which day follows Shrove Tuesday?
2. In which country was the Battle of Waterloo fought in 1815?
3. The world's biggest toyshop is in London's Regent Street. What is it called?
4. Which newspaper, now over 200 years old, was nicknamed 'the Thunderer'?
5. In which game were Babe Ruth and Hank Aaron famous players?
6. Which female detective moved from *The Gentle Touch* to *C.A.T.S. Eyes*?
7. What nationality is Sophia Loren, the film star?
8. Which composer associated with Aldeburgh was given a life peerage in 1976?
9. What is the chemical symbol for magnesium?

54

1. The Queen's official cars have no number plates.
2. The warming pan.
3. Alaska.
4. . . . *Robinson*.
5. Cricket.
6. *The Archers*.
7. Dick Turpin.
8. The double bass.
9. The sheep.

142

1. Ash Wednesday.
2. Belgium.
3. Hamley's.
4. *The Times*.
5. Baseball.
6. Maggie Forbes, played by Jill Gascoigne.
7. Italian.
8. Benjamin Britten.
9. Mg.

1. If a person dies intestate, what has he omitted to do?
2. Which king of Britain went mad, so that his son was made regent in 1811?
3. In which city are the Latin quarter and the Sorbonne?
4. In which novel by Charles Dickens does the burglar Bill Sykes appear?
5. Which soccer team plays home matches at Ninian Park?
6. Which pair of animals are the best-known cartoon creations of William Hanna and Joseph Barbera?
7. Whose catch-phrase is, 'You'll like this – not a lot, but you'll like it!'?
8. Whose first British number one hit was 'It's Not Unusual'?
9. What is a Lhasa Apso?

1. What do too many cooks spoil, according to the proverb?
2. Who was Henry VIII's last wife?
3. Where is America's bullion kept?
4. Where was the court of King Arthur?
5. For what did King Constantine of Greece win an Olympic gold medal?
6. Who was the male star of the film *Grease*?
7. Who accompanied Sherpa Tensing to the top of Mount Everest?
8. Which is the lowest of these voices in singing: bass, contralto, tenor and baritone?
9. What colour is jet?

55

1. Make a will.
2. George III, who died in 1820.
3. Paris.
4. *Oliver Twist*.
5. Cardiff City – 'the Bluebirds'.
6. Tom and Jerry.
7. Paul Daniels.
8 Tom Jones.
9. A dog.

143

1. The broth.
2. Catherine Parr.
3. Fort Knox.
4. Camelot.
5. Yachting – Dragon Class.
6. John Travolta.
7. Sir Edmund Hillary, in 1953.
8. Bass.
9. Black.

Who accompanied Sherpa Tensing . . . ?

1. What do Britons call the American 'gas' or gasoline?
2. During which war did the Battle of the Bulge take place?
3. Which is the largest river basin in the tropical world?
4. How many birds in the bush is one in the hand worth?
5. Over how many days is the Olympic decathlon held?
6. Who plays June in *Terry and June* on TV?
7. Whose motto is 'Nation shall speak peace unto nation'?
8. Which pop group had a hit with 'Pass the Dutchie'?
9. Who discovered radium?

1. What metal are people said to be as bold as?
2. Which fleet was overwhelmingly defeated in 1588?
3. Of which Caribbean island is Port of Spain the capital?
4. What did the Ancient Mariner kill?
5. Who was the goal-keeper of Italy's team that won the 1982 World Cup?
6. What's the title of the 1985 Muppet film, set in New York?
7. What did the humorist Edward Lear teach Queen Victoria to do?
8. In which Gilbert and Sullivan operetta does Little Buttercup appear?
9. George Stephenson invented locomotives, but what did Robert Stevenson invent that has saved many lives?

56

1. Petrol.
2. The Second World War.
3. The Amazon river basin.
4. Two.
5. Two.
6. June Whitfield.
7. The BBC.
8. Musical Youth.
9. Pierre and Marie Curie.

144

1. Brass.
2. The Spanish Armada.
3. Trinidad.
4. The albatross.
5. Dino Zoff.
6. *Muppets Take Manhattan*.
7. Draw – he was a very good artist.
8. *HMS Pinafore*.
9. The flashing light for lighthouses at sea.

1. What are mascherone, bel paese and roquefort?
2. Which battle was fought at Battle?
3. Where is the Blarney Stone?
4. How many knights made up the Order of the Round Table?
5. What was tennis player Maureen Connolly's nickname?
6. What sort of animal was Dumbo?
7. What's the magazine produced by the Consumers' Association to advise people on best buys?
8. To which once popular group did Debbie Harry belong?
9. Who wrote a book about the forces and rules of motion called *Principia Mathematica*?

1. People at dances who don't get partners are called by what floral name?
2. Who was the first king of England after the Commonwealth period?
3. Which country's emblem is the thistle?
4. Who was told by a soothsayer to 'beware the Ides of March', but was still murdered?
5. Of what are modern vaulting poles made?
6. Which musical film about Annie Oakley starred Betty Hutton and Howard Keel?
7. For his ownership of what is Rupert Murdoch famous?
8. Under what sort of tree did the jolly swagman camp, in 'Waltzing Matilda'?
9. What precious stones are often used in lasers?

57

1. Kinds of cheese.
2. No, not the Battle of Battle – the Battle of Hastings, 1066.
3. At Blarney Castle, County Cork, Ireland.
4. 150.
5. Little Mo.
6. An elephant.
7. *Which?*
8. Blondie.
9. Sir Isaac Newton.

145

1. Wallflowers.
2. Charles II.
3. Scotland.
4. Julius Caesar – Ides of March meant 15 March.
5. Fibreglass.
6. *Annie Get Your Gun.*
7. Newspapers, like *The Times* and the *Sun*.
8. Coolabar.
9. Rubies.

1. Which airline uses a koala bear as its symbol?
2. Who said, 'I think that he who prays best will fight best'?
3. What is the capital of China?
4. Who wrote about Roberta, Peter and Phyllis in *The Railway Children*?
5. Which trophy in which sport was named after Dwight F. Davis of Harvard?
6. In the TV series *Callan* what part did Russell Hunter play?
7. For what was Beau Brummell noted?
8. Which Osmond sang the hit 'Long-haired Lover from Liverpool'?
9. How many teeth have fully grown dogs and bears?

1. From which country do BMW cars come?
2. The Ming dynasty of the fourteenth and fifteenth centuries occurred in which country?
3. For what do the initials USSR stand?
4. Who created Tarzan?
5. At which field event did Viktor Saneyev win three Olympic gold medals?
6. What is Mr Magoo's first name in the cartoon?
7. What sort of animal was Sir Alfred Munnings famed for painting?
8. Paul Humphreys and Andy McCluskey belong to OMD, but what's the band's full name?
9. From what does cork come?

58

1. QANTAS, from Australia.
2. Oliver Cromwell.
3. Peking.
4. E. Nesbit.
5. Lawn tennis's Davis Cup.
6. Lonely – he was called that because he smelled terrible!
7. His very elegant clothes.
8. Little Jimmy Osmond.
9. Forty-two.

146

1. Germany.
2. China.
3. Union of Soviet Socialist Republics.
4. Edgar Rice Burroughs.
5. Triple jump (previously called hop, step and jump).
6. Quincy.
7. The horse.
8. Orchestral Manoeuvres in the Dark.
9. The bark of the cork tree.

*Its bark is worse
than its bite!*

1. In the nursery rhyme, what ran away with the spoon?
2. Which English cathedral was badly burnt in July 1984?
3. Where is the Golden Gate Bridge?
4. In the fairy tale, who could spin straw into gold?
5. In which sport would you use halyards and spinnakers?
6. Who is Barney Rubble's next-door neighbour?
7. What is the maximum score possible with one dart?
8. Which musical contains the song 'Matchmaker, Matchmaker'?
9. Which British fish with three spines build nests on the bottoms of ponds to hatch their young?

1. How many winks is a short sleep?
2. What fabled city of gold was sought by Spanish explorers, mainly in the sixteenth century?
3. In which country is the Order of St Olaf awarded?
4. In the Bible, which of the disciples tried to walk on water?
5. What's the minimum number of darts needed to score exactly 501, ending on a double?
6. Speedy Gonzales is the fastest mouse – where?
7. Which British seaside resort has a Golden Mile?
8. Which singer had a backing group called the Wailers?
9. If you took a Rorschach test, what would you be looking at?

59

1. The dish.
2. York Minster.
3. San Francisco Bay.
4. Rumpelstiltskin.
5. Yachting.
6. Fred Flintstone.
7. Sixty – treble twenty.
8. *Fiddler on the Roof*.
9. Sticklebacks.

147

1. Forty.
2. El Dorado.
3. Norway.
4. Peter.
5. Nine.
6. In all Mexico.
7. Blackpool.
8. Bob Marley.
9. Ink blots.

1. What is the ninth month of the year?
2. What was the motto of the French Revolution?
3. Which character in *Quincy* shares his name with Japan's highest mountain, an extinct volcano?
4. From what was Cinderella's coach made?
5. By what name is Edson Arantes do Nascimento better known?
6. Where on television could you see Harold Cross and Damon Grant?
7. Which member of the Royal Family is President of the Save the Children Fund?
8. Who is the patron saint of mountaineers and is associated with animals that save people lost in snow?
9. Which plant with the name of a planet catches flies?

1. How many engines does Concorde have?
2. Who said, on learning that she was to be queen of England, 'I will be good'?
3. In which ocean is Hawaii?
4. Who was the first king of the Israelites?
5. On which sport do Nigel Starmer-Smith and Bill McLaren commentate for television?
6. Who was Tarzan's chimpanzee friend?
7. To whose band did Alan-a-Dale belong?
8. How many fiddlers had Old King Cole?
9. What sort of stone floats on water?

60

1. September.
2. 'Liberty, equality, fraternity'.
3. Fujiyama. Sam Fujiyama is played by Robert Ito.
4. A pumpkin.
5. Pelé.
6. Characters in Channel 4's *Brookside*.
7. Princess Anne.
8. St Bernard.
9. Venus fly trap.

148

1. Four – they're Rolls-Royce Bristol Olympus 593 engines.
2. Queen Victoria.
3. The Pacific.
4. Saul.
5. Rugby union.
6. Cheetah.
7. Robin Hood's merry men.
8. Three.
9. Pumice stone.

1. In which country are Ferrari cars built?
2. The third Duke of Richmond established which racecourse in Sussex?
3. Bergen and Stavanger are towns in which country?
4. In Greek mythology, how was Adonis killed?
5. Which sports organization is the ABA?
6. By what name is the comedian Fred Scuttle better known?
7. Which organization's motto is, 'Fidelity, bravery, integrity'?
8. Who built the first music synthesizer in the 1960s?
9. What medical breakthrough was Dr Christiaan Barnard the first to perform in 1967?

1. For what medal do the letters DFC stand?
2. In which city did the Easter Rising start a revolution in 1916?
3. Which is the world's largest tourist attraction that doesn't have free admission?
4. Which alphabet that sounds like a man's name is used to write Russian and Bulgarian?
5. In which event in 1984 did Zimbabwe win its first Olympic gold medal?
6. Who on TV plays the Bounder?
7. What type of sleeve takes its name from the earl who led the British forces in the Crimea?
8. In which film does Elvis Presley appear as a ghost?
9. Some animals aestivate when it's hot. What does 'aestivate' mean?

61

1. Italy.
2. Goodwood.
3. Norway.
4. By a wild boar while out hunting.
5. The Amateur Boxing Association.
6. Benny Hill.
7. The Federal Bureau of Investigation.
8. Robert Moog, hence the Moog synthesizer.
9. The first heart transplant.

149

1. Distinguished Flying Cross.
2. Dublin.
3. Disneyland.
4. Cyrillic.
5. Women's hockey.
6. Peter Bowles.
7. Raglan.
8. *Love Me Tender*.
9. Sleep or rest, just as other animals hibernate when it's cold.

1. Beginning with l, what is the legal word for theft?
2. The Normandy landings of June 1944 were known by what code name?
3. Which American city is known as 'the Big Apple'?
4. Which king in the Bible saw the writing on the wall?
5. Who scored the most runs in the 1984 Test Match series for England against the West Indies?
6. In *E.T.*, how many brothers did Gertie have?
7. If your hobby involved looking for fritillaries, what would you probably be collecting?
8. Who was John Lennon's wife at the time of his death?
9. Which fruit is called 'Nature's toothbrush'?

1. In a leap year, during which month is the extra day?
2. In 1783, who became prime minister of Britain at the remarkably early age of twenty-four?
3. Of which country is The Hague the capital?
4. What does 'The Bible' literally mean?
5. Which Austrian was the 1984 Formula I world champion racing driver?
6. Which TV serial tells the story of a group of doctors and their patients?
7. Appropriately named, who was the first to fly over both the North and South Poles?
8. Which character sings 'When You Wish Upon A Star' in Walt Disney's *Pinocchio*?
9. What does the name 'dandelion' mean?

62

1. Larceny.
2. Overlord.
3. New York.
4. Belshazzar.
5. Alan Lamb – 386 in total.
6. Two.
7. Butterflies – you'd be a lepidopterist.
8. Yoko Ono.
9. The apple.

150

1. February.
2. William Pitt (the younger, of course!).
3. Holland.
4. The book.
5. Niki Lauda, who also won in 1975 and 1977.
6. *The Practice*.
7. Admiral Richard Evelyn Byrd.
8. Jiminy Cricket.
9. Tooth of the lion (French: *dent de lion*).

1. Which is the middle colour on traffic lights?
2. Which part, or parts, of a person were put into the stocks, an old form of punishment?
3. The White Sea is off the coast of which country?
4. Which stories did Laura Ingalls Wilder write about where she grew up in the American West?
5. With which sport is Cowes connected?
6. John Schneider, Tom Wopat and Catherine Bach appear in which fast-moving American TV series?
7. How many white squares are there on a chessboard?
8. What did the straw man want in *The Wizard of Oz*?
9. From which animal do we get venison?

1. How many sides has a 20-pence piece?
2. Mary Tudor said, 'When I am dead, you will find the word . . . written on my heart.' To which place was she referring?
3. What is the capital of Hawaii?
4. How many lines are there in a sonnet?
5. What does the hammer weigh in field athletics?
6. Who is Supergran's constant enemy, played on TV by Iain Cuthbertson?
7. In which country was Florence Nightingale born?
8. *Vox angelica*, *bourdon* and *dulciana* are parts of which musical instrument?
9. In which part of your body would you feel a migraine?

63

1. Amber.
2. Their legs.
3. The USSR, to the north.
4. *The Little House on the Prairie* and several others that became a TV series.
5. Yachting.
6. *The Dukes of Hazzard.*
7. Thirty-two.
8. A brain.
9. The deer.

151

A sport for Cowes?

1. Seven.
2. Calais.
3. Honolulu.
4. Fourteen.
5. 16 lbs, or about 7.25 kg.
6. The Scunner Campbell.
7. In Italy – in the city of Florence!
8. A full-sized organ.
9. In your head.

1. In the nursery rhyme, what did the three little kittens lose?
2. What was New York's Idlewild Airport renamed in the 1960s?
3. Stamps bearing the letters RSA come from which country?
4. The phrase 'chapter and verse' originally referred to what?
5. Which game is played at Twickenham?
6. What is the full name of Dave Starsky's partner, called Hutch for short?
7. To what position was John Masefield appointed in 1930?
8. Whose body lies 'a-mouldering in his grave' in the song?
9. A camel has the same number of stomachs as an octopus has hearts – how many?

1. Which company made the Model T car, then the Model A?
2. In 1871 much of Chicago was burnt down. What started the fire?
3. Which store in London's Knightsbridge is often thought of as the world's finest?
4. Which spectacular birds pulled Juno's chariot?
5. How many attempts at each height may a pole vaulter take?
6. On which island is the detective series *Bergerac* set?
7. What invention did Steven Perry patent in 1845 that holds things together?
8. Rouget de Lisle composed the French national anthem, which is called what?
9. Which creature can hold its breath longest?

64

1. Their mittens.
2. John F. Kennedy Airport.
3. Republic of South Africa.
4. Finding the exact location of something in the Bible.
5. Rugby union.
6. Ken Hutchinson (or perhaps Kenneth).
7. Poet Laureate.
8. John Brown's.
9. Three.

152

1. Ford.
2. A cow kicked over a lantern in its barn.
3. Harrods.
4. Peacocks.
5. Three.
6. Jersey.
7. Elastic bands.
8. 'La Marseillaise'.
9. The whale.

'. . . thirty-eight thirty-nine, forty . . .'

1. Who lives at Gatcombe Park?
2. In ancient times, people of which country worshipped cats?
3. What is the capital of Scotland?
4. At the end of a letter, for what do the letters PS stand?
5. In which country did golf originate?
6. In the comedy film *The Silver Streak*, starring Gene Wilder, who or what is the Silver Streak?
7. How many pieces are needed to block a point in backgammon?
8. Which line precedes 'Long live our noble Queen' in the British national anthem?
9. Approximately what percentage of the body's weight is the skin?

1. In Australia, what are sundowners?
2. General Louis Botha was the first premier of which country?
3. Convicts used to be sent to Botany Bay – where is that?
4. Who was the fattest pupil at Greyfriars School?
5. Which Derby winner was kidnapped from an Irish stud farm?
6. In 1985, who partnered Michael Sundin and Simon Groom on *Blue Peter*?
7. What are the three primary colours?
8. What's the first note on the tonic sol-fa scale?
9. Why is red cedar a good lining for storage boxes and closets?

65

1. Princess Anne and her family.
2. Egypt.
3. Edinburgh.
4. Postscript, or *postscriptum* (Latin).
5. Scotland.
6. A fast long-distance train.
7. Two.
8. 'God save our gracious Queen'.
9. 5 per cent.

153

1. Tramps.
2. South Africa.
3. Australia, near Sydney.
4. Billy Bunter.
5. Shergar.
6. Janet Ellis.
7. Red, blue and yellow.
8. Doh.
9. Because it repels moths.

1. What's the more usual name for the infection called tetanus?
2. What was the capital of the ancient country of Assyria?
3. In which country would you be most likely to find a *geisha*?
4. Ali Baba's magic phrase was 'Open sesame!' What is sesame?
5. Who was the first English footballer to be transferred for £1 million?
6. Who played the headmistress, Miss Fritton, in the St Trinian's films?
7. What did the American George Horace Gallup originate in the 1930s?
8. Who was born first – J. S. Bach, Haydn, Beethoven or Brahms?
9. Which tree in Australia is called the ghost gum?

1. For what do the letters ILEA stand? (As a clue, the organization runs a large number of schools.)
2. On which ship with the name of a breed of dog did Charles Darwin sail to South America on his expedition?
3. In which county is Windsor Castle?
4. Who asked for John the Baptist's head as a reward for her dancing?
5. In which sport was Neil Adams world champion?
6. Which New York street is famous for its theatres?
7. In a rainbow, which colour is next to red?
8. Which Englishman composed the opera *Dido and Aeneas* and is buried in Westminster Abbey?
9. Which is the most common blood group?

66

1. Lockjaw.
2. Nineveh.
3. Japan.
4. A type of cereal or grain.
5. Trevor Francis.
6. Alistair Sim (dressed as a woman).
7. Opinion polls.
8. J. S. Bach was born first, in 1685.
9. The eucalyptus.

154

1. Inner London Education Authority.
2. The *Beagle*.
3. Berkshire.
4. Salome.
5. Judo.
6. Broadway.
7. Orange.
8. Henry Purcell.
9. O.

1. In Morse code, a full stop is the same as which letter repeated three times?
2. In which country did the civil wars called the Frondes take place?
3. Which country contains the world's largest silver mine, at Broken Hill?
4. What's the name of the hunchback of Notre Dame?
5. Which team finished top of the Rugby league in 1984?
6. Which animal plays a very important part in the British film *A Private Function*?
7. What was the painter Whistler's first name?
8. First violin, second violin, cello and double bass – what is missing from the string section of a symphony orchestra?
9. By what name is the *Ursus horribilis* more familiarly known?

1. How many sides has a pentagon?
2. Who was the first man to cross the Niagara Falls on a tightrope?
3. Which major river flows between New York and New Jersey?
4. According to the proverb, if two's company what is three?
5. For what do the letters lbw stand in cricket?
6. At which game is the film star Omar Sharif an international player?
7. Which chess piece can move only diagonally?
8. If you add one letter to lute, which other musical instrument can you make?
9. In rocketry, what do the letters ICBM represent?

67

1. A – it's dot-dash-dot-dash-dot-dash.
2. France.
3. Australia.
4. Quasimodo.
5. Hull Kingston Rovers.
6. Betty the pig.
7. James.
8. Viola.
9. Grizzly bear.

155

Two's company, three's a . . . ?

1. Five.
2. Charles Blondin.
3. The Hudson.
4. A crowd.
5. Leg before wicket.
6. Bridge.
7. The bishop.
8. Flute.
9. Inter-Continental Ballistic Missile.

68

1. At what time did the mouse run down the clock in the rhyme?
2. Which Persian king was defeated at Marathon?
3. Which famous obelisk, shipped from Egypt, stands on London's Embankment?
4. Which author wrote *Redgauntlet* and *The Heart of Midlothian*?
5. Which team plays home matches at Goodison Park?
6. Which sergeant in a classic TV comedy series is stationed at Fort Baxter?
7. Who was the last Viceroy of India?
8. Who composed 'The Young Person's Guide to the Orchestra'?
9. If you had the letters FRCVS after your name, what would your occupation probably be?

156

1. Which month is often called 'flaming'?
2. In 1777, which general lost the Battle of Brandywine?
3. Which river does the world's longest suspension bridge span?
4. The spoiling of what started the battle between Tweedledum and Tweedledee?
5. Where are the Oaks and the Derby run?
6. In *Hi-De-Hi*, who owns the holiday camp in which the series is set?
7. Who has owned yachts called *Morning Cloud*?
8. Which pop group was the first to be awarded the MBE?
9. Prunes are dried versions of which fruit?

1. One o'clock.
2. Darius.
3. Cleopatra's Needle.
4. Sir Walter Scott.
5. Everton.
6. Ernie Bilko (played by Phil Silvers).
7. Lord Louis Mountbatten.
8. Benjamin Britten.
9. Veterinary surgeon.

156

1. June.
2. George Washington.
3. The Humber.
4. A rattle.
5. Epsom racecourse.
6. Joe Maplin.
7. Edward Heath.
8. The Beatles.
9. Plums.

Flaming June

69

1. What is an intermediate floor between two floors of a building called?
2. What fruit did Nell Gwyn sell?
3. In which mountain range is the Matterhorn?
4. Who wrote *The Guns of Navarone* and many other thrillers?
5. In which sport do you use a foil on a piste?
6. Which TV comedy series features a pop singer and his piano teacher, Belinda Purcell?
7. What nationality was the polar explorer, Roald Amundsen?
8. Which concert hall stands opposite the Albert Memorial in London?
9. How many arms have two dogs, two cats and six chickens?

157

1. How many years make a century?
2. Which German general was known as the Desert Fox?
3. Which country's capital is Rabat?
4. How many letters are there in the English alphabet?
5. How many form a competition tug-of-war team?
6. Which TV comedy series starred Paul Nicholas and Jan Francis as Vince and Penny?
7. Which street in London is famous for selling diamonds?
8. Who composed the 'Fingal's Cave' overture, and was called Felix?
9. How many eyelids has a snake?

69

1. Mezzanine.
2. Oranges.
3. The Alps.
4. Alistair Maclean.
5. Fencing.
6. *Roll Over Beethoven*.
7. Norwegian.
8. The Royal Albert Hall.
9. None.

157

1. One hundred.
2. Erwin Rommel.
3. Morocco. The word Rabat means 'small town'.
4. Twenty-six.
5. Eight.
6. *Just Good Friends*.
7. Hatton Garden.
8. Mendelssohn.
9. None.

1. What is the main ingredient of Coca-Cola?
2. Which king was nicknamed 'the Unready'?
3. From which London station would you catch a direct train to Glasgow?
4. In which book of the Bible are the Ten Commandments first written?
5. In which game do you have scrums?
6. From what ailment does Mr Magoo suffer?
7. Which great popular singer was nicknamed 'the Old Groaner'?
8. At which time of the year would you be most likely to sing carols?
9. What does a filly grow up to be?

1. For what does VIP stand?
2. Who was Britain's longest-serving Member of Parliament?
3. Through where did Lady Godiva ride naked?
4. What was William Shakespeare's middle name?
5. In which sport might someone hold you in a half-nelson?
6. Who is Bruce Wayne's assistant?
7. Who was appointed Poet Laureate in December 1984?
8. What follows Doh, Ray, Me, Fah, . . . ?
9. Raisins are dried – what?

70

1. Water.
2. Ethelred.
3. Euston.
4. Exodus.
5. Rugby.
6. Bad eyesight.
7. Bing Crosby.
8. At Christmas.
9. A mare.

In which sport do you have scrums?

158

1. Very Important Person.
2. Sir Winston Churchill.
3. The streets of Coventry.
4. He didn't have one!
5. Wrestling.
6. Dick Grayson (Robin) – Bruce Wayne is Batman, of course!
7. Ted Hughes.
8. Soh, La, Ti, Doh.
9. Grapes.

1. On which British coin are the Prince of Wales' feathers shown?
2. Who was the Sailor King and ruled Britain immediately before Queen Victoria?
3. Why are there thirteen stripes on the American flag?
4. Which author created *The Hobbit* and then wrote *Lord of the Rings*?
5. In the game of bridge, how many cards does each player get to start a game?
6. Which art expert on TV introduced the character of Morph?
7. Which cartoon character's favourite muscle-building food is spinach?
8. Which pop group was named after a prison in Berlin?
9. If a digital clock says 22:49, how many minutes are there left before midnight?

1. What do the British call the garment known to Americans as a vest?
2. In ancient Rome, what was the difference between patricians and plebeians?
3. In which county are Lands End and St Ives?
4. Which famous horror story about a scientist making a monster was written by Mary Shelley?
5. In which games do players normally wear a waistcoat but no jacket?
6. What's the name of the grey cat who regularly appears on *Blue Peter*?
7. In 1984 Dr David Jenkins became Bishop of where?
8. Who formed Wings after leaving his original super-group?
9. What are always kept 1.453 metres or 4 feet 8½ inches apart – a distance known as 'standard gauge'?

71

1. The 2p piece.
2. William IV.
3. They represent the thirteen original states that made up the USA.
4. J. R. R. Tolkien.
5. Thirteen – the whole pack is dealt out between four people.
6. Tony Hart.
7. Popeye.
8. Spandau Ballet.
9. Seventy-one.

159

1. A waistcoat.
2. Patricians were nobles, plebeians were the common people.
3. Cornwall.
4. *Frankenstein*.
5. Snooker and billiards.
6. Jack.
7. Durham.
8. Paul McCartney.
9. Railway lines.

1. If you subtract six dozen from half a gross, what's left?
2. What did Henry Ford say that history was, more or less?
3. Which country uses punts for money?
4. In the rhyme, which Jack could eat no fat?
5. What does a toxophilite aim at?
6. Which film was the sequel to *The Guns of Navarone* and also had 'Navarone' in its title?
7. Which stately home would you visit to see the National Motor Museum?
8. Which top solo singer was previously with the Streetband, then with the Q-Tips?
9. Where in your body is your Achilles tendon?

1. A nervous or anxious person may be said to be like a cat on what?
2. Which country once had a class of powerful warriors called *samurai*?
3. What was the African country of Zimbabwe formerly called?
4. Who wrote the series of books that begin with *The Lion, the Witch and the Wardrobe*?
5. What do the initials of the cricket organization MCC represent?
6. In which comedy series would you see Foggy, Compo and Clegg?
7. What is listed in a Stanley Gibbons catalogue?
8. Which musical instrument has a chanter, drones and an air sack?
9. What's the ordinary name for ferrous oxide, a reddish, crumbly substance?

72

1. Nothing – they're both seventy-two.
2. 'History is more or less bunk.'
3. The Irish Republic.
4. Jack Sprat.
5. An archery target, with arrows.
6. *Force Ten from Navarone*.
7. Beaulieu.
8. Paul Young.
9. In or just above your heel.

160

1. Hot bricks.
2. Japan.
3. Rhodesia.
4. C. S. Lewis.
5. Marylebone Cricket Club.
6. *Last of the Summer Wine*.
7. Postage stamps of the world and their selling prices.
8. Bagpipes.
9. Rust.

1. Why should you keep careful watch on a kleptomaniac?
2. Which President of the USA had the same name as a vacuum cleaner?
3. Which country's flag is white with a red circle in the centre?
4. What's the more usual name for the religious group called the Society of Friends?
5. Which British girl won the javelin event in the 1984 Olympic Games?
6. What does Doctor Who call his spaceship?
7. In what sort of building would you find a green room which may not be green at all?
8. Curt Smith and Roland Orzabal make up which successful pop group?
9. What's the name of a factory in which crude oil is turned into petrol?

161

1. What special name is used for a fox's tail?
2. Who became dictator of Spain after the Spanish Civil War?
3. What's the word used for the book in which a record of a ship's voyages is kept?
4. Which poet's birthday do Scots celebrate on 25 January each year?
5. Geoff Hunt and Jahangir Khan have both won the world championship in which sport?
6. Which TV series tells you about the Ewing family?
7. Which artist is famous for having cut off his own ear?
8. Which Englishman composed *Let's Make An Opera*, *Noye's Fludde* and *Peter Grimes*?
9. If beef comes from a cow, what do we call the meat from a calf?

73

1. A kleptomaniac is a compulsive thief who can't help stealing.
2. Herbert Hoover.
3. Japan.
4. The Quakers.
5. Tessa Sanderson.
6. The Tardis.
7. In a theatre, TV studio, or concert hall.
8. Tears for Fears.
9. It's called a refinery.

161

1. Brush.
2. General Francisco Franco.
3. The log.
4. Robert Burns.
5. Squash.
6. *Dallas*.
7. Vincent van Gogh.
8. Benjamin Britten.
9. Veal.

1. Where would you see an ISBN, and what is it?
2. What did ancient Britons do with woad?
3. What's the only county in England whose name begins with an A?
4. Who wrote the set of long poems called *The Canterbury Tales*?
5. In what does an archer keep his arrows?
6. Which jungle-dweller's story was told in the 1984 film *Greystoke*?
7. On what special board does an artist mix his paints?
8. Which pop group with a brief name first made it to the top of the charts with 'Red Red Wine'?
9. If a doctor's a gerontologist, what does he specialize in?

1. Who lives in a manse?
2. The ruined city of Knossos was the capital of Minoan civilization on which Mediterranean island?
3. Denmark has a border with only one other country. Which one?
4. What reward was Judas Iscariot given for betraying Jesus?
5. From which wood are cricket bats made?
6. In which TV comedy series does Paul Shane play Ted Bovis and Ruth Madoc play Gladys Pugh?
7. In which part of London's Hyde Park do crowds of people gather to hear orators speak on all sorts of subjects?
8. Where in London are the Promenade concerts held?
9. Which planet has the same name as Mickey Mouse's pet dog?

1. International Standard Book Number – which you see printed in most published books.
2. They painted themselves blue with it.
3. Avon.
4. Geoffrey Chaucer.
5. A quiver.
6. Tarzan.
7. A palette.
8. UB40.
9. Treating old people.

1. A clergyman.
2. Crete.
3. West Germany.
4. Thirty pieces of silver.
5. Willow.
6. *Hi-De-Hi.*
7. At Speakers' Corner.
8. The Royal Albert Hall.
9. Pluto.

1. What are Barlinnie, Long Lartin and Parkhurst?
2. Who was known as the Maid of Orleans?
3. Which island south of Australia has Hobart as its capital?
4. In the Bible, who used the jawbone of an ass to kill a thousand men?
5. Which sport do you associate with Newton Abbot, Ripon and Fontwell Park?
6. Which Baron is the enemy of Dangermouse?
7. Who has been question master of *University Challenge* since 1962?
8. Which singer who usually wears a hat and sunglasses had a big hit with 'Happy Talk'?
9. What's the national flower of Wales?

163

1. What colour is a postage stamp costing 2 pence?
2. Which liner sank after hitting an iceberg in 1912?
3. In which country is Bantry Bay?
4. Which book by George Orwell tells the story of a revolution led by Napoleon, Snowball and other pigs?
5. Henley and Holme Pierrepont are places connected with which sport?
6. Which television hero was played by Michael Praed, then by Jason Connery?
7. In the game of chess, which pieces are placed in the corners at the start of the game?
8. What sort of music would you hear at Glyndebourne in Sussex?
9. Which instrument do submariners use to see above the water when submerged?

75

1. Prisons.
2. Joan of Arc.
3. Tasmania.
4. Samson.
5. Horse racing.
6. Baron Greenback.
7. Bamber Gascoigne.
8. Captain Sensible.
9. Daffodil, *not* leek, which is a vegetable.

163

1. Green.
2. The *Titanic*.
3. The Irish Republic.
4. *Animal Farm*.
5. Rowing.
6. Robin Hood, in *Robin of Sherwood*.
7. Rooks, or castles.
8. Opera.
9. A periscope.

1. What does a chiropodist look after?
2. Nicholas II and his wife Alexandra were the last royal rulers of which country?
3. Which city is the capital of Argentina?
4. Who wrote *Gumble's Yard*, *Widdershins Crescent* and *Noah's Castle*?
5. In which sport is there an annual competition called the Indianapolis 500?
6. Who starred in the first of the 'spaghetti westerns', *A Fistful of Dollars*?
7. What was invented by Sir Frank Whittle?
8. What's the first name of Rogers Nelson, from Eden Prairie, Minneapolis, that he uses when he sings?
9. Argon, helium, krypton, sodium, neon – which one isn't a gas?

1. What are schipperke, papillon and weimaraner?
2. Who was the first English printer?
3. What was the former name of the island of Sri Lanka?
4. In which Shakespeare play do Puck, Bottom and Oberon appear?
5. Which sport would you be watching if you saw a flying camel or a triple salchow?
6. Where would you meet Gobo, Red, Wembley and Sprocket the dog?
7. Who followed Konstantin Chernenko as leader of the USSR?
8. What do Jill Bryson and Rose McDowall call themselves on discs like 'Since Yesterday' that suggests a fruit knife?
9. What sort of fish can be made into kippers?

76

1. People's feet.
2. Russia.
3. Buenos Aires.
4. John Rowe Townsend.
5. Motor racing.
6. Clint Eastwood.
7. The jet engine.
8. Prince.
9. Sodium, which is a metal.

164

1. Breeds of dog.
2. William Caxton.
3. Ceylon.
4. *A Midsummer Night's Dream.*
5. Ice skating.
6. *Fraggle Rock.*
7. Mikhail Gorbachov.
8. Strawberry Switchblade.
9. The herring.

A sporting camel?

1. What do we call the process of making a detailed count of Britain's population, which is done every ten years?
2. Who was exiled first to Elba, then to St Helena?
3. Where will you find the San Andreas Fault?
4. Which comedian wrote *Adolf Hitler: My Part in his Downfall* and *Silly Verse For Kids*?
5. James Hunt was the last Briton to be world champion at what?
6. In which TV series do Percy Sugden and Mavis Riley appear?
7. What is Mrs Margaret Thatcher's middle name?
8. Which two Phils had a hit with 'Easy Lover' in 1985?
9. From its name what do you know that a vertebrate animal possesses?

1. What word is used for a bed on board ship?
2. Which explorer sailed from Bristol to discover Newfoundland in 1497?
3. Into which ocean does the Amazon River flow?
4. What name is used for the book in which a cartographer's work is printed?
5. In which sport are competitors required to find their own way round a course, using a map and compass?
6. On which day of the week is the TV quiz *Bullseye* transmitted?
7. What was the surname of Groucho, Chico and Gummo?
8. On a violin, what's the small piece of wood that holds the strings away from the body of the instrument?
9. What would you measure in bels or decibels?

77

1. The census.
2. Napoleon Bonaparte.
3. In California – it's an earthquake zone that passes through San Francisco.
4. Spike Milligan.
5. Motor racing – he was top driver in 1976.
6. *Coronation Street*.
7. Hilda – she was born Margaret Hilda Roberts.
8. Phil Collins and Philip Bailey.
9. A backbone. The word vertebrate stems from 'vertebra', the name of the sections of bone which make up the spine.

165

1. A bunk, or perhaps a hammock.
2. John Cabot.
3. The Atlantic.
4. An atlas – he draws maps.
5. Orienteering.
6. Sunday.
7. The Marx Brothers
8. The bridge.
9. Volume of sound.

Orienteering?

78

1. What do the British call the hat known in the USA as a derby?
2. As what was the Black Prince known when he became king of England?
3. On which river does the city of Vienna stand?
4. What title was used for John Christopher's three science fiction books, *The White Mountains*, *The City of Gold and Lead* and *The Pool of Fire*, when they were televised?
5. In which sport could you do a slalom and an Eskimo roll?
6. Who makes the A-Team 'look like a bunch of fairies' because she's 'got more bottle than United Dairies'?
7. In the British peerage, what is an earl's wife called?
8. 'Breakin' My Heart' was a hit for which singer who sounds a little wobbly?
9. Which tiny creatures do ants keep for their milk, as humans keep cows?

166

1. What number is one-third of three-quarters of twenty-four?
2. Which explorer's first names were Robert Falcon?
3. What's the name of the large fortress which stands next to Moscow's Red Square?
4. Who is regarded as the patron saint of children?
5. In which Olympic sport must competitors swim, shoot, ride, fence and run?
6. In which TV series does Rex Smith play Jesse Mach, rider of a super-fast motorbike?
7. If you looked after guppies and mollies, what would your hobby be?
8. Which group told us 'Everybody Wants To Rule The World'?
9. In 1955, Jonas Salk made a vaccine to help fight which disease?

78

1. Bowler hat.
2. He never succeeded to the throne as he died young, and his son became Richard II.
3. The Danube.
4. *The Tripods*.
5. Canoeing.
6. Supergran, in the title song.
7. She is a countess.
8. Shaky, or Shakin' Stevens.
9. Aphids.

166

1. Six.
2. Captain Scott of the Antarctic.
3. The Kremlin.
4. St Nicholas, or Santa Claus.
5. Modern pentathlon.
6. *Street Hawk*.
7. Keeping tropical fish.
8. Tears for Fears.
9. Poliomyelitis, often shortened to 'polio'.

1. The Victoria Cross is the highest British award for bravery; what's the second highest?
2. Who led an expedition with three ships – the *Nina*, the *Pinta* and the *Santa Maria*?
3. What does *auf Wiedersehen* mean?
4. Which women in legend sat on rocks and sang so beautifully that they lured sailors to shipwreck and death?
5. In which sport would you see holeshots and burnouts at Santa Pod?
6. In which TV programme can we catch up on events in Albert Square?
7. Who was the last bachelor to be prime minister of Britain?
8. Which famous singer who was made a Dame of the British Empire is best remembered for singing 'We'll Meet Again' during the Second World War?
9. Thomas Alva were the first names of which great inventor?

1. Which rank in the army sounds like the inside of a nut, but is spelt differently?
2. For which nation that fought against Rome was Hannibal a general?
3. On either side of which narrow stretch of water are the Pillars of Hercules?
4. In the proverb, what do empty vessels make?
5. In 1984, Robert Millar was Scottish sportsman of the year – for which sport?
6. Which magician asks the questions on *Odd One Out*?
7. Who is the mother of Miss Zara Phillips?
8. 'Every Time You Go Away' was a hit for which singer?
9. Which ginger-bearded broadcaster is an expert on botany?

79

1. The George Cross.
2. Christopher Columbus.
3. Goodbye, or, until we meet again.
4. Sirens.
5. Drag racing – motor-car racing over a quarter-mile from a standing start.
6. *EastEnders*.
7. Mr Edward Heath, 1970–74.
8. Vera Lynn.
9. Edison.

Lured to a watery grave

167

1. Colonel – sounds like kernel.
2. Carthage.
3. The Straits of Gibraltar.
4. The most noise.
5. Cycling.
6. Paul Daniels.
7. Princess Anne.
8. Paul Young.
9. David Bellamy.

1. *Sois prêt* is the French version of the Boy Scout motto. What is it in English?
2. Since the Civil War, who is the only British monarch to have ruled for less than a year?
3. Which country was ruled by a Shah until the Ayatollah Khomeini took over?
4. In Longfellow's poem, why did Paul Revere take a night-time ride on horseback in 1775?
5. Which film about athletes in the 1924 Olympic Games won four Oscars in 1981?
6. Which actor has played both Doctor Who and Worzel Gummidge?
7. Which German city gave its name to 'a square meal in a round bun'?
8. Who starred in the rock movie *Purple Rain* with his band, the Revolution?
9. What is unusual about a grasshopper's ears?

1. What does London's Billingsgate market specialize in selling?
2. What used to be called LSD?
3. What special manufacturing plant was moved from London to Llantrisant in South Wales in 1968?
4. Who wrote *A Dog So Small* and *Tom's Midnight Garden*?
5. In the Olympics, women used to compete in the pentathlon of five events, but what is it called now that it has seven events?
6. Which character in *Coronation Street* runs a clothes factory?
7. Which actor played Frank Spencer in *Some Mothers Do 'Ave 'Em*, and starred in the stage musical *Barnum*?
8. Which great opera singer has an ice-cream named after her?
9. Where in the human body would you find rod cells and cone cells?

1. 'Be Prepared'.
2. Edward VIII, from January to December 1936.
3. Iran.
4. To warn that the British were coming.
5. *Chariots of Fire*.
6. Jon Pertwee.
7. Hamburg – to the hamburger, but in Hamburg, people call it a 'whopper'.
8. Prince.
9. They're in its legs!

1. Fish.
2. Money – the letters stood for pounds, shillings and pence before decimalization.
3. The Royal Mint, where coins are made.
4. Philippa Pearce.
5. Heptathlon.
6. Mike Baldwin.
7. Michael Crawford.
8. Dame Nellie Melba – the ice-cream is Peach Melba.
9. In the eye.

1. Which is the 'merry month'?
2. Who was born in Burnham Thorpe in Norfolk and became a famous admiral?
3. A wok is mainly used for cooking food originating from which country?
4. Who rules Wonderland in Lewis Carroll's book?
5. What is one stroke over par called in golf?
6. Norman Stanley Fletcher was locked up in which prison in *Porridge*?
7. Which comedian is called 'the Rochdale Cowboy'?
8. Who, according to legend, lured Rhine sailors to their death with her singing?
9. Of what is ornithology the study?

1. How many people make up a jury in English courts?
2. Which country has been ruled by Sancho the Fat and Pedro the Cruel?
3. What unofficial title is given to the wife of the President of the USA?
4. Which creature did Alice follow into Wonderland?
5. How many play on a volleyball team?
6. In which store is Captain Peacock the floorwalker?
7. With what is Robert Carrier chiefly associated?
8. If you are lucky enough to own a Stradivarius or an Amati, what do you have?
9. What does a gosling grow up to be?

81

1. May.
2. Horatio Nelson.
3. China.
4. The Queen of Hearts.
5. Bogey.
6. Slade.
7. Mike Harding.
8. Lorelei.
9. Birds.

169

1. Twelve.
2. Spain.
3. The first lady.
4. The White Rabbit.
5. Six.
6. Grace Brothers, in *Are You Being Served?*
7. Cooking and food.
8. A very old, very valuable violin.
9. A goose or a gander

1. What did the Three Bears have for breakfast?
2. Of which Red Indian tribe was Geronimo the chief?
3. After which city in India is a type of riding trousers named?
4. Who wrote *The Children of the New Forest*?
5. In July 1984 who was appointed manager of Barcelona Football Club?
6. In which TV series is part of the show called 'Speak Easy'?
7. Thomas Sheraton was famed for making what?
8. With what type of music is Louis Armstrong associated?
9. According to legend, which bird delivers babies?

1. What is the Indian style of clay-oven cooking called?
2. Which prime minister was nicknamed Dizzy?
3. 'Space City' is the nickname of which Texas town?
4. Who wrote the long poems *Paradise Lost* and *Paradise Regained*?
5. How many runs are scored in a maiden over?
6. What kind of animal is Roobarb in the TV cartoon series?
7. In 1984 Dom Mintoff resigned as Prime Minister of which country?
8. In the song 'Oh Susannah!', what does the man from Alabama have on his knee?
9. Which blood-sucking African fly can infect humans with sleeping sickness?

82

1. Porridge.
2. The Apache.
3. Jodhpur.
4. Captain Marryat.
5. Terry Venables.
6. *CBTV*.
7. Furniture.
8. Jazz – he played the trumpet.
9. The stork.

170

1. Tandoori.
2. Benjamin Disraeli.
3. Houston.
4. John Milton.
5. None.
6. A dog.
7. Malta.
8. A banjo.
9. The tsetse fly.

The dizzy heights of No 10

1. What does PAYE stand for?
2. According to legend, who drove all the snakes from Ireland?
3. From which Moroccan port does the tangerine take its name?
4. Who wrote the original Dracula novel?
5. How many play in a netball team?
6. Who asked the questions on *We Love TV*, the quiz about television?
7. Which Duke's home is Arundel Castle?
8. Which of the following was *not* a great composer: Mozart, Mendelssohn, Marlowe, Mahler?
9. In which continent might you see zebras and giraffes in the wild?

1. On which everyday object do you find the words *decus et tutamen*?
2. How many new pence is the old florin worth?
3. In New York's Manhattan, which avenue divides the east side from the west side?
4. Who was 'the Demon Barber of Fleet Street'?
5. Which bird's name is also the nickname of Brighton and Hove Albion Football Club?
6. Which actress plays Arthur Daly's wife in the TV series *Minder*?
7. Which is the last colour to be potted at snooker?
8. What is the pitch of the lowest string on a violin?
9. What is a young hare called?

83

1. Pay As You Earn.
2. St Patrick.
3. Tangier.
4. Bram Stoker.
5. Seven.
6. Gloria Hunniford.
7. The Duke of Norfolk.
8. Marlowe – he was a playwright.
9. Africa.

171

1. Round the edge of a £1 coin.
2. Ten.
3. Fifth Avenue.
4. Sweeney Todd.
5. The seagull(s).
6. Nobody – the character never appears.
7. Black.
8. The G below middle C.
9. A leveret.

1. Which country's embassy in London did the SAS storm after a siege in 1980?
2. Which queen reputedly said, 'Let them eat cake'?
3. Which is Britain's longest river?
4. Who wrote *Lord of the Flies*?
5. Who attempted to jump Snake River Canyon on a 'skycycle'?
6. Who was the first Doctor Who?
7. Who is second in line to the throne?
8. How many strings has a viola?
9. Which animal is called 'the ship of the desert'?

1. When is St Swithin's day?
2. Which Scot got his inspiration from a spider?
3. From where does a Mancunian come?
4. In the Bible, who was Jacob's first wife?
5. How many soccer teams are there in the English second division?
6. On which quiz programme are Bill Beaumont and Emlyn Hughes the team captains?
7. Which comedian originally became famous by imitating a police car and saying, 'Nick, nick'?
8. What is a bongo?
9. What is a black widow?

84

1. It was the Iranian Embassy.
2. Marie Antoinette.
3. The Severn.
4. William Golding.
5. Evel Knievel.
6. William Hartnell.
7. Prince William.
8. Four.
9. The camel.

172

1. July 15th.
2. Robert the Bruce.
3. Manchester.
4. Leah.
5. Twenty-two.
6. *A Question of Sport*.
7. Jim Davidson.
8. A drum, but it's also a kind of antelope.
9. A spider.

1. Where on your body would you wear a fez?
2. What is the present-day name of East Pakistan, now a separate country?
3. In which country is Snowdon?
4. Who wrote *The Fourth Protocol* and *The Day of the Jackal*?
5. What was Don Bradman's game?
6. Who presents *That's Life*?
7. In a rainbow, which colour comes between yellow and blue?
8. From which country does the rumba originate?
9. Which organ of the body does the disease hepatitis affect?

1. How many months are there in five years?
2. In 1883, what happened at Krakatoa?
3. Who is the patron saint of Wales?
4. Who or what frightened Miss Muffet away?
5. In which game are goal defence and wing attack two of the positions?
6. Which Jim will fix it?
7. How many tricks are needed for a small slam at bridge?
8. Which leader of the group called the Comets had one of the first rock'n'roll hits with 'Rock Around the Clock'?
9. Which creatures live in dens called holts?

85

1. On your head.
2. Bangladesh.
3. Wales.
4. Frederick Forsyth.
5. Cricket.
6. Esther Rantzen.
7. Green.
8. Cuba.
9. The liver.

173

1. Sixty.
2. Possibly the biggest eruption and earthquake in history
   – Krakatoa is a volcano.
3. St David.
4. The spider.
5. Netball.
6. Jimmy Savile.
7. Twelve.
8. Bill Haley.
9. Otters.

1. Which organization's flag shows the world seen from above the North Pole, with a wreath of olive branches around it?
2. What name was used for the Norsemen from Scandinavia who raided all over Europe between the eighth and eleventh centuries?
3. Into which inland sea does the River Volga flow?
4. Which popular children's author wrote *Black Hearts in Battersea*, *Wolves of Willoughby Chase* and *The Cuckoo Tree*?
5. In which of the Japanese martial arts do competitors fight with bamboo swords?
6. Which TV series told the story of a group of women held prisoner by the Japanese?
7. From which country does Indian ink originally come?
8. Which pop singer's real surname is Panayiotou?
9. What Christmas novelty did Tom Smith, a London baker, invent in the 1840s that his company still makes?

1. Which method of code communication uses two flags?
2. Which Italian city has a world-famous leaning tower?
3. In London it's called the Underground. What is it called in Paris?
4. Who ate honey from the carcass of a dead lion, and made a riddle about it?
5. If you belonged to the Tope Club of Great Britain or the British Casting Association, what would your hobby be?
6. Which 1962 classic film about a desert hero starred Peter O'Toole and Omar Sharif?
7. Which film star wrote *The Moon's a Balloon* and *Bring on the Empty Horses*?
8. Holly, Paul, Nasher, Pedro and Mark make up which group?
9. How many pips are there in the Greenwich time signal?

1. The United Nations.
2. The Vikings.
3. The Caspian.
4. Joan Aiken.
5. Kendo.
6. *Tenko*.
7. China.
8. George Michael of Wham!
9. Christmas crackers.

174

1. Semaphore.
2. Pisa.
3. The Métro.
4. Samson, in the Bible (Judges 14:14).
5. Fishing or angling.
6. *Lawrence of Arabia*.
7. David Niven.
8. Frankie Goes to Hollywood.
9. Six – five short and one long.

1. *Per ardua ad astra* is the motto of which of the armed forces?
2. Who is said to have stated the law of gravity after an apple fell on his head?
3. In which city is O'Hare Airport, the world's busiest?
4. In H. G. Wells's novel *The War of the Worlds*, which two worlds were at war?
5. Which sport holds its world championship at the Crucible Theatre in Sheffield?
6. Which film monster was shot down by aeroplanes as he climbed up the Empire State Building?
7. Which worldwide movement began with a ten-day camp on Brownsea Island, Poole, in 1907?
8. Who sang 'Congratulations' in the Eurovision Song Contest in 1968?
9. Who or what lives in an eyrie?

1. If someone told you they were travelling by shanks's pony, what would they mean?
2. In which war did the Charge of the Light Brigade take place?
3. What's the capital of India?
4. Which British newspaper holds the record of ninety-seven misprints in one story only 5½ column inches long?
5. In which city is Headingley Test cricket ground?
6. Which ITV company has its headquarters in Manchester?
7. Which famous Spanish artist painted the 'Rokeby Venus', which is in London's National Gallery?
8. What's the nickname of singer Stephen Duffy, a member of Duran Duran in the early days?
9. Which animal is said to weep when it eats its unfortunate victims?

87

1. The Royal Air Force.
2. Sir Isaac Newton.
3. Chicago: 43 million passengers passed through it in 1983.
4. The Earth and Mars – Mars lost . . .
5. Snooker.
6. King Kong.
7. The Boy Scout Movement.
8. Cliff Richard.
9. An eagle.

175

1. That they would be walking.
2. The Crimean War.
3. Delhi.
4. *The Times*, on 22 August 1978, in a story about the Pope.
5. Leeds.
6. Granada.
7. Diego Rodriguez de Silva y Velasquez (1599–1660) – just Velasquez will do!
8. Tintin.
9. The crocodile.

1. Who compiled the first English dictionary?
2. Which international organization, set up in 1920, was replaced in 1946 by the United Nations?
3. In which country is Cape Trafalgar, near which the Battle of Trafalgar was fought in 1805?
4. Who wrote about Malory Towers School and the O'Sullivan twins at St Clare's?
5. Which Olympic event has Sebastian Coe won twice?
6. In the TV comedy series *Dad's Army*, what was the correct name of the 'army'?
7. Which sport would you expect to hear Kent Walton describe on TV?
8. From which country does 'penillion' singing come?
9. What's the name of the University of Manchester's large radio telescope at a site in Cheshire?

1. Groups of what are called covens?
2. In 1946, what did Winston Churchill call the border between Eastern European countries and the West?
3. Which mountain range is said to be the home of the yeti?
4. In Roald Dahl's book *The BFG*, who is the BFG that Sophie meets?
5. What wooden object is not allowed to be more than 96.5 centimetres long or 10.8 centimetres wide (38 inches by 4¼ inches)?
6. At the end of which television programme is Biddy Baxter named as editor?
7. Who wrote the world's longest-running stage play, *The Mousetrap*?
8. Which group took 'I Want to Know What Love Is' to the top of the British hit parade?
9. Why don't polar bears eat penguins?

1. Dr Samuel Johnson.
2. The League of Nations.
3. Spain, near the Straits of Gibraltar.
4. Enid Blyton.
5. The 1,500 metres.
6. The Home Guard.
7. Wrestling.
8. Wales.
9. Jodrell Bank.

1. Witches.
2. The Iron Curtain.
3. The Himalayas – it's another name for the Abominable Snowman.
4. Big Friendly Giant.
5. A cricket bat.
6. *Blue Peter*.
7. Dame Agatha Christie.
8. Foreigner.
9. Polar bears live near the North Pole, and penguins near the South Pole. Of course, perhaps they can't get the silver paper off the Penguins . . .

Why don't polar bears eat Penguins?